What people are saying

CHURCH ZERO

"Church planting in the way of the apostles ... that's what Peyton is trying to recover. And nothing less will do. We both sense the profound significance of the recovery of a missional ministry for an apostolic church. A good contribution in a critical time."

Alan Hirsch, founder of Forge Mission Training Network and Future Travelers and author of *The Permanent Revolution* (with Tim Catchim) and numerous other books on missional movements

"*Church Zero* is a bold and exciting call for us to become the church that God has always dreamed! Peyton Jones writes in a way that will not only inform you but energize you to lead a new breed of church. If you love church planting like I do, read this book, and buy it for a church planter!"

Dave Ferguson, author of *On The Verge* and *Exponential* and Visionary for NewThingGrace

"*Church Zero* is a fresh read in a tired category of church books. Peyton paints a picture of how God builds a church around the faithful lives of simple people and simple practices."

Hugh Halter, author of *The Tangible Kingdom, Sacrilege,* and *AND: The Gathered and Scattered Church*

"If you are hungry to serve the Lord and His church, have a deep love for God's Word, and desire to make an impact for Jesus Christ, then this book is for you. Peyton Jones clearly articulates the importance of the fivefold gifts for ministry and how they should function in the church today. This well-written, provocative book should be read by everyone who is serious about the fulfillment of the Great Commission."

Jeff Schwarzentraub, senior pastor of
Harvest Bible Fellowship of Denver
and president of One Heartbeat

"Peyton Jones has a passion for Christ's church. *Church Zero* is a call to churches everywhere to wake up, try new things, and get out of the four walls to reach the world."

Brian "Head" Welch, former guitarist for Korn

"*Church Zero* dishes out the mutha of all wedgies to fake, fruitless, impotent Christianity and sets out a compelling biblical blueprint for a new breed of church that might just unleash the kind of gospel ruckus that Jesus always intended."

Dai Hankey, cofounder New Breed Church
Planting and author of *Offensive* and *Hard Corps*

"I have to admit, I got hung up reading this book. I am spurred on, filled with the fires of possibility. This is probably the best biblical study on what an apostle looks like today. Reading this book made me feel like we really can take our land as the 'little *a* team.' New Breed *is* getting out there and getting it done. It *is* the

Very Old School meets Very New School: so simple it's radical. It *is* DIY, trust-the-Lord-and-launch-with-abandon kinda stuff. It is a brazen contrast to everything showy and flashy. Let's take the gospel outside the city. Let's fulfill the Great Commission. Use this book as your soul's kindling … and *burn it down*!"

Josh Brindle, Tribe of Judah Ministries
and Calvary Chapel Iron River, MI

"Soldiers coming off the front lines of the battlefield bring home a no-nonsense, unsurpassable perspective when it comes to distinguishing between what actually works and noneffective armchair philosophies. In the same way we have here Peyton Jones—a true soldier for Christ—with the real-world experience to command our attention as he calls the twenty-first-century church to action. It's time to wake up out of the slumber, pick up our soldiers-for-Christ kitbag, and get ready to move as we model the forgotten, timeless, battle-tested tactics of the first-century church!"

Chad Williams, US Navy SEAL

CHURCH ZERO

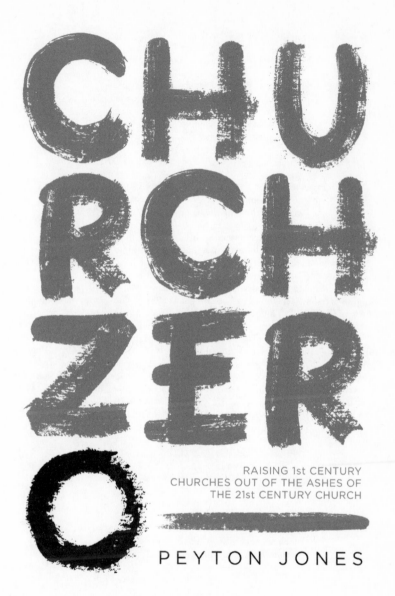

CHURCH ZERO

RAISING 1st CENTURY
CHURCHES OUT OF THE ASHES OF
THE 21st CENTURY CHURCH

PEYTON JONES

David C Cook®

transforming lives together

CHURCH ZERO
Published by David C Cook
4050 Lee Vance View
Colorado Springs, CO 80918 U.S.A.

David C Cook Distribution Canada
55 Woodslee Avenue, Paris, Ontario, Canada N3L 3E5

David C Cook U.K., Kingsway Communications
Eastbourne, East Sussex BN23 6NT, England

LCCN 2013930732
ISBN 978-1-4347-0493-1
eISBN 978-0-7814-0880-6

© 2013 Peyton Jones

The Team: Alex Field, Karen Lee-Thorp, Amy Konyndyk,
Nick Lee, Caitlyn Carlson, Karen Athen
Cover Design: Micah Kandros Design

Printed in the United States of America
First Edition 2013

1 2 3 4 5 6 7 8 9 10

012713

ACKNOWLEDGMENTS

First, thanks to David Ollerton, whose *Ministry on the Move* planted many seeds.

Next, Eric Fulmer brought me to faith; Peter Warren discipled me; and my first preaching and ministry mentor, Dan Berg, recognized the call of God upon my life (you're partly to blame). Although he's been a furniture repairman for most of his ministry, Dan has an uncanny mastery of the lost gift of illustration and is the breathing embodiment of Spurgeon's John Ploughman. Also, Bill Welsh is my sending pastor, my church-planting partner, and an awesome model of a sold-out ex-Jesus-hippy who still wants to conquer the world for Jesus. Last but not least, Charlie Marquez is my stateside number-two punk and the Cuba Gooding Jr. to my Jerry Maguire. Thank you all.

Thanks also to my Welsh Compadres. Dai Hankey, M.C. massive church preaching legend and thuggy bald man who first listened to my crazy ideas when I was cooking up New Breed and who signed his name to the two-punks-and-a-logo idea. Without him, it would have been one punk and no logo, and I'd never have gotten this far. Jan Jensen, the first church planter I jumped with. Peter Jeffery, my second mentor who showed me what anointed Spirit-filled preaching was and that I was just playing in the whitewash. And Len and Margaret Gibbs, my Welsh parents, who fed my body at the table while planting the corrupting seeds into my mind.

Jeff Roberts is a wizened sage and ex-church-planter whose prophetic gifting and father's heart couldn't have come at a better time.

Thanks for leading me patiently into the deeper things of the Spirit. I'll miss you most of all, scarecrow!

Then there are the dead guys: C. H. Spurgeon, David Martyn Lloyd-Jones, and Bob Kane.

And the not-dead crew: Francis Chan, Alan Hirsch, Dave Ferguson.

And my agent, Steve Laube, the "John Carter" of Arizona.

And all at the David C Cook family: Don Pape and Alex Field for championing my cause.

And my editor, Karen Lee-Thorp: the flux capacitor of her editing skills can only be compared to Doc Brown making the DeLorean fly through time using Marty Mcfly's household garbage.

Finally, Andrea, my wife, is the often unrecognized, uncredited church-planting partner who fell in love with me, supported me, followed me, partnered with me, dreamed with me, risked with me, and makes this whole church-planting thing look good. I beat ya to the book thing!

CONTENTS

When a paradigm shifts, everyone goes back to zero.
Joel Barker

1
THIS IS GONNA HURT

Having begun by the Spirit, are you now being perfected by the flesh?

Paul, Galatians 3:3

*Christianity has achieved apparent success by
ignoring the precepts of its Founder.*

H. Richard Neibuhr

How long? Not long. 'Cause what you reap is what you sow.

Rage Against the Machine, *Wake Up*

Size matters not.

Master Yoda

There I was, sitting in a room in Wales, the most unchurched part of the United Kingdom, gearing up to hear the pastoral wisdom of Francis Chan. I don't know how they got him to come to this place, of all the crummy gin joints in the world, but there he was, kicking down his radical manifesto to a crew of pastors who were very clearly not getting what he was driving at. Francis was speaking about his unconventional move to leave his thriving California megachurch, travel to the developing world, and visit the underground Chinese church in hopes of radically rethinking what church was meant to be. Free-falling into the hands of God, he was on a mission of discovery to scrape together some paradigm of ministry that he could believe in: something that nurtured discipleship, was less self-serving to the pastor, and had more practical impact.

And that's when it happened.

He said he had begun to wonder if there was something missing in our current setup. Then he dropped the A-word (and it ain't[1] what you're thinking).

Apostle.

It's the new A-bomb in church circles.

It's a word that's used in nearly every book in the New Testament, and yet twenty-first-century Christians dodge it like Superman recoiling from kryptonite. As it echoed in the vacuum of stunned silence, the hackles rose on the nape of my neck. I thought, *Holy New Testament vocabulary, Batman! This guy is going to blow the doors off the church if he keeps dropping the biblical A-bomb!*

The word *apostle* had become like the ark of the covenant to me, and lately I was feeling the contrast between the pastoral Dr. Jones's mundane routine of charming the ladies with stuffy indoor academic-type pulpit lectures and the alter-ego adventurer Indy inside me, desperately trying to break out. When reading the book of Acts, I'd often ask myself, "Why does what we do in ministry today look so different from the way Paul did it?" I'd been rediscovering the biblical role of the apostle for the last few years, and I realized that Francis had been brought to my doorstep so that he could be used to deliver a divine kick up my backside by being so bold as to use that word. The end result was me chaining myself to my desk and writing about what I'd begun to witness in Europe.

For over a decade I'd been involved in various forms of church planting in Wales as an overseas tent-making missionary pastor. The oldest Celtic-speaking nation and once known as "the land of revivals," Wales has become the forgotten part of the UK. Hugging the western rim of northwestern Europe alongside Ireland, Wales also represents the cutting edge of postmodernism. When I first set foot on Welsh terra firma twelve years ago, I could see that it wasn't going to be easy. Almost immediately I slammed into two important facts: first, the secular ethos and post-Christian mind-set were swallowing churches alive in the UK like the mighty Sarlacc pit's digestive juices slowly eroding Boba Fett's Mandalorian body armor. Second, I was going to have to completely relearn ministry from the foundations up if I was going to get anywhere in this God-forsaken mission field.

Those two realizations made me desperate. In the natural world, desperation creates a fight-or-flight reflex. In the spiritual realm, it's not too different. The second you realize that it's either sink or swim, the adrenaline starts to juice you up, and you get radical. Fighting isn't usually my first instinct; *flighting* is. Nonetheless, I've always been the kind of guy who was willing to do anything, no matter how crazy it sounded, or how scared I was, as long as I knew God was in it.

I can relate to Gideon. I understand all of his hesitation and boldness in alternating steps. That's usually the cadence of my footsteps as well. Although I may not like it at the time, most often I'll eventually drag myself to the electric chair, reluctantly strapping in with Thomas's helpless but sarcastic words ringing in my head: "Let us also go, that we may die with him" (John 11:16).

I had been called by God to make an impact in a culture that saw less than 1.6 percent of the population attending church—and I had to change. The way I did ministry had to change. So I started reading the Bible a bit more....

Oh yeah, and I started paying more attention to the book of Acts.

THE NEW TESTAMENT WORD FOR MISSIONARY

Let me ask you: doesn't it seem weird that our missionary manifesto, the New Testament, lacks the word *missionary* in the English translations? Think about that.

Can that be right?

On the contrary, my dear Watson, the word you've been looking for has been under your nose all along. It *is* there. You just haven't recognized it because of how it has been translated. It's the word *apostle*. *Apostolos* in the Greek means "sent one" and can be translated as "missionary."

Now what did the New Testament missionaries do? They planted churches.

What if all the buzz about church planting and missional church wasn't something new that plaid-clad, horn-rimmed-glasses-wearing hipsters had invented, but rather something that was inherent in the word *apostolos*?

Before the A-bomb sends you running for cover, screaming what a freak I am, let me assure you that I mean apostle with a little a. I don't mean a guy with superpowers or somebody who still writes Scripture in his spare time. Nor am I a member of the Apostolic denomination.

Bear with me.

Most people out there believe the term *apostle* belongs exclusively to the Twelve. True, the Twelve were "sent ones," but the New Testament term *apostle* is not exclusively used for the Twelve. Once Paul used *apostle* to describe his role, there were thirteen, but did you know that the Greek word *apostolos* is used for nine other individuals in the New Testament as well? Oh yeah, it is, but the English translators rendered it as *messenger* or *representative* because it didn't gel with their theology to translate it literally from *apostolos* to apostle.

What if the church had a theological blind spot that was obstructing a biblical theology of church planting?

What the translators fail to understand is that the New Testament knows two different types of apostles. The first group was known as "the Twelve." They were capital-A Apostles and missionaries to the twelve tribes of Israel, and they were never to be replicated or replaced. They were handpicked by Jesus for a specific time in history. The second category—little-a apostles—was a lesser group of church planters who served under Paul. He gave them the title of apostolos. The word apostolos is definitely used for the Twelve, as in Matthew 10:2, but not for them alone. The word is also used for Paul, and he wasn't one of the Twelve. Here are nine other people called apostles (*apostolos*, plural: *apostoloi*) in the New Testament, none of whom were part of the Twelve:

- Titus (2 Cor. 8:23)
- James, the Lord's brother, not John's brother from Club 12 (Gal. 1:18–19)
- Barnabas (Acts 14:14)
- Apollos (1 Cor. 4:6–9)
- Andronicus (Rom. 16:7)
- Junias (Rom. 16:7)
- Epaphroditus (Phil. 2:25)
- Timothy (1 Thess. 1:1–2:6)
- Silas/Silvanus (1 Thess. 1:1–2:6)

Those are just the ones Paul mentioned. Paul worked with a network of missionaries who were also sent out by Jesus on a frontline, life-or-death church-planting commando recon mission. In fact, Paul used the title of *apostle* for what he did in church planting: "for he who worked through Peter for his apostolic ministry to the circumcised worked also through me for mine to the Gentiles" (Gal. 2:8). He said to the Corinthians, "Are you not my workmanship in the Lord? If to others I am not an apostle, at least I am to you, for *you* are the seal of my apostleship in the Lord" (1 Cor. 9:1–2). A paraphrase of that could be, "If to others I am not a 'sent-out one,' at least

I am to you, for you are a proof or validation of my 'sent-out-ness' in the Lord." His apostleship was proved by the fact that the Corinthian church existed. Why? Because apostle = church planter.

The lesser apostles didn't meet the same criteria as the Twelve, nor were they leaders over the whole church. Instead, these lesser apostles operated as church-planting missionaries. There may be a parallel between the lesser apostles and the seventy-two disciples that Jesus sent out. Although these disciples didn't have special status or authority, their role was nonetheless to spread the word to villages and towns that needed to hear. Paul was not one of the Twelve, but he was a kind of link between the twelve apostles who were there from the beginning and those who would take his place: Timothy, Titus, and the others.

This makes sense of why, in Ephesians 4, Paul said apostles (and prophets and evangelists) are necessary for building up the church alongside pastors and teachers. Paul spoke of them as if they were commonplace.

True, there are those who say, as I once believed, that the roles of apostle and prophet faded into oblivion upon the completion of Scripture. In the modern church, however, we've managed to exterminate teacher and evangelist as well so that we're left with the pastor-only model. What if, as a result of amputating these roles, the church were a dismembered quadriplegic? Would that explain why it isn't moving? Would it shed light on why the church inchworms pathetically on its mission like a fat little grub?

If we ignore the biblical roles Christ gave us to accomplish the mission, then our structure will be wrong. If the structure is wrong, then the functionality will be limited. If the functionality is limited, then our mission will be compromised. If our mission is compromised, we won't be as effective as Jesus intended.

We have been ignoring these important roles to our peril. The Western church is beginning to wake up to the reality that with all the sound and fury of our success, we've lost something. This has happened throughout history. Did you know that it's possible for a society to go backward in its understanding? An entire civilization can devolve technologically and lose vital stratagems for engineering because they've forgotten certain methods.

For example, the Romans knew how to make fifty-foot-high hydraulic cement aqueducts that spanned valleys. If you go to modern Britain, you will still see their ruins towering against the backdrop of impossible landscapes. Centuries later, however, the engineers of the Dark Ages couldn't replicate these feats because they'd lost the Roman technology to make structural cement. What if the church has lost vital biblical technology essential to advancing the kingdom of Christ? Like medieval Europe, we'd be scratching our scalps, wondering how they did it in the past, yet we'd be hindered from making real progress ourselves.

The church planting network that I run may be called New Breed, but you're probably beginning to piece together that we're really kicking it old school. Like, two-thousand-years-old school. If the church recovers the apostolic-style ministry that made the first century tick, then it will jump-start the church back to the threatening force that it was two thousand years ago. Like Indiana Jones uncovering the ark of the covenant in the Well of Souls, we need to unearth the divine technology that has lain hidden in the depths of God's Word all along.

Before we do, let's look at the current weakened structure of Western evangelicalism.

FORMULAS FOR DISASTER

Francis Chan's dissatisfaction with the current model of evangelical hierarchy is only the beginning of the shakedown that is happening in Western Christianity. It points to cracks in our foundation.

The emergent movement began with disenchantment with the evangelical megachurch movement in America, where many of them ran like big-business enterprises. Here are the nuts and bolts of the machine broken down from the instruction manual:

How to Build a Megachurch in Five Easy Dance Steps

1. Get more people
2. More people = more money
3. More money = more toys
4. More toys = more ways to get more people
5. Get more people (rinse and repeat)

This is the model that has been used for decades in America, but to what aim? Many young men in leadership during the 1990s stood at the top of the megachurch pyramid, rolled their idle crowns on their index fingers, and muttered, "Now what?"

After the emergent movement dissed the megachurch movement, dissidents of evangelicalism flocked to these churches that put the "hip" in discipleship. When the emergent churches became "successful" in numbers, they simply reproduced what they had come from—except that now people did finger painting to punk music onstage. As history repeated itself, the emergent leaders sat on thrones built out of solid cool, forlorn with chin in palm, asking the familiar question, "Now what?" Thus history repeateth.

Why did the early church that had seen so many conversions and changed the first-century landscape not face this same problem?

Well, it almost did.

Picture yourself in Jerusalem at the dawn of the apostolic age, circa Acts 3. You had given up everything once you discovered God's sacrificial lamb. Now you sat at the feet of eleven guys who were ordinary just like you, yet extraordinary. Ordinary fishermen and tradesmen, they were transformed, like you, by an encounter with Jesus of Nazareth. Their ministry was so powerful that you never wanted to leave their teaching or the warm fellowship of the community, or the fear and awe-tinged miracles that buzzed the atmosphere with supernatural power.

It had all the makings of a megachurch experience: thousands of people, money to do anything they wanted, and ministry coming out of their ears. There was only one problem. The kingdom couldn't advance in a holy huddle. God had to give them a spiritual kick up the backside.

Enter Saul of Tarsus. Persecution smacked down on the church like Gallagher's twenty-five-pound sledgehammer on a watermelon, splattering the seeds of the church to the far reaches of Asia Minor. If the church wouldn't go out willingly, they'd be scattered unwillingly. That is God's time-tested method of getting His people to heed the Great Commission. In Europe today, postmodernism has been forcing churches to venture outside to reach the unreached. There is desperation in leaders who have realized that it's either sink or swim.

Pioneer third-world missionary C. T. Studd once said:

> Some want to live within the sound
> Of Church or Chapel bell
> I want to run a Rescue Shop
> within a yard of hell.[2]

The churches that won't heed Jesus's call to get out there will die—and in fact are already dying from within. This isn't just happening in Great Britain. The dry rot in America has already set. We're just repeating Britain's pattern fifty years later. In the 1950s in Britain, the churches were full, packed with families. Preaching legend Peter Jeffery recalls how on the streets of Britain in the fifties, an open-air preacher would draw folks out of their front doors, toting folding chairs so they could listen. In the sixties, however, the sexual revolution put the church to bed, and the youth slowly trickled out of the church scene. Nobody panicked. Do you know why? The churches were still relatively full. One decade, two decades later, and the silver heads woke up to the widening maw of an irreversible generation gap as they literally died off one by one. As the numbers in the church graveyard increased, the numbers in the pews decreased. When they woke up to the shrinking church— evidenced by the empty pews—the panic finally broke out. But by then it was too late.

When I returned to the United States after being abroad for twelve years, the first thing I noticed was that we'd lost the youth on a Sunday.

Nobody is worried; the numbers are still big.

Wait ten years.

Churches that depend on their size tend to rest on their laurels. That's what happened in the early church. When the book of Acts closes, the Holy Spirit leaves us with an important message. Megachurch Jerusalem had faded to the narrative background and ceased to be an influential presence in the world. Instead, the focus of Acts is on the smaller, nondescript churches that were springing up in the most remote parts of the map. The kingdom was clawing its way outward, fighting for every inch of pagan ground taken.

The expanding church was apostolic, and that made it vibrant and dangerous. Impossible to ignore. So much so that we still look back at it for inspiration. But have we put its principles into practice?

I'm not opposed to megachurches. Please believe me. Overnight, God created the first megachurch in Jerusalem at Pentecost, but I don't think we're learning the lessons that God intended by studying their example. The megachurch model can be useful, but it can also provide a huge hurdle to kingdom expansion if the model is more concerned with bringing people in than sending people out. Let's face it—that was largely the trend in the eighties and nineties.

Megachurches in the book of Acts, like Jerusalem in the early days—and Antioch and Ephesus—were biblical sending agencies, mission powerhouses. This is what God designed megachurches to be. Ever wonder who planted the seven churches of Asia? Acts 19:10 indicates that Paul used the megachurch at Ephesus as a church planting hub while he trained the planters daily in the school of Tyrannus: "This continued for two years, so that all the residents of Asia heard the word of the Lord." Rick Warren models the right use of megachurch might by using Saddleback's accumulated money, influence, and energy to establish gospel work in every nation on earth. In the past twenty years, Warren has become a multi-church planting machine, equipping and empowering young people to plant around the globe. Likewise, my personal hero is my sending pastor in Huntington Beach. A reluctant megachurch pastor and true missionary at heart, he vowed in the 1990s to break the trend and send his best guys to the mission field without fail. Anyone who stays behind is repeatedly told that they are left behind to—you guessed it—help send others out.

The irony is that only leaders who have the priority of sending people out will foster the type of church that will continue to bring people in. You have to be willing to lose your life if you want to find it.

NOBODY USES AN EIGHT-TRACK ANYMORE

When I was a kid, people still had turntables for vinyl records (they hadn't discovered mixing yet). They also had an eight-track.

I've lost half of you....

It was supposed to be the next big thing. The problem was that somebody came up with a better format that made the eight-track obsolete. The church keeps rolling out formats that are supposed to bring the next big wave of some kind of wonderful. Like the eight-track, they get dated, lose steam, and are forgotten. Some of you reading this are actually saying, "Oh yeah, the eight-track. Forgot about that."

Eight-tracks didn't replace vinyl, but they opened the door for other formats. They gave way to cassette tapes, cassette tapes to CD, CD to digital mp3. Likewise, the church has replaced one format with another over the years, seeking to reinvent itself without questioning whether the next big thing is biblical. The end result is always the same. We've changed the format without revolutionizing the church into a time-tested format. As a result, we can't even remember the previous formats that the apostles laid down for us.

The church is trying to play the eight-track tape of church to an iTunes world.

What if there was a time-tested model in the Bible? What if it was laid out in the book of Acts, but we missed it because it doesn't fit our church structure? What if the next big thing is going back to the biblical methodology? If God drew up the battle plan for us two thousand years ago, why do we feel the need to draft another one?

It's time for us to go back to the future.

ACTS OF THE CHURCH PLANTERS

Most of our modern books about church tell us how to do church. The book of Acts never does this. It never offers us a model of church that guarantees success if we follow the template. I would have thought that the basic "power principles" of church growth and dynamics would have been found there, not in a book by some author who lives in today's anemic church culture. But Acts surpasses culture and time by refusing to provide a model and instead lists basic core components that every healthy church should have: breaking of bread, sharing with those in need, continuing in teaching, meeting together often, praying, and so on (2:42). But it never goes any further than that in telling us how to have a church service. Isn't that a bit strange?

That depends on your assumption of what Acts was written for.

Was Acts written to show pastors how to make church good, or was it written to show how the kingdom of God expanded through church planting? The more I read the Acts of the Apostles, the more I'm convinced that it's the script of the first-century version of *How the West Was Won*.

Maybe God isn't so concerned about what the church looks like on the ground as long as those things in Acts 2:42 are all present. Maybe what God is more concerned about is that we understand how the kingdom expanded effectively through church planting so that we don't merely hobble along in obedience to the Great Commission. If the Holy Spirit chose to invest great detail in a record of how churches got planted in a pagan world (against impossible odds), we'd be fools to ignore His advice. Like I mentioned earlier, New Breed isn't very new. It's really old school. It's just not been done like that for a long time. New Breed Church Planting is using the time-tested method, tried and true by the apostles, abandoned only when the church became "successful" in the fourth century.

In roughly ten years of church planting, Paul was able to say in Romans 15:19 "that from Jerusalem and all the way around to

Illyricum I have fulfilled the ministry of the gospel of Christ." Did you catch that? Paul considered that he'd fulfilled his mission in Asia Minor. Having fulfilled that task, he could now move on to another area where Christ hadn't been named.

Ten years, and a minimum of fourteen church plants later, and Paul was done.[3] Why can't we do this today? In trying to expand the kingdom of heaven, what on earth have we been missing?

CHURCH PLANTING IN BLACK AND WHITE

This is basically what church planting has looked like for a long time. Rod Sterling of *Twilight Zone* appears from the shadows and narrates what we've been watching for the past few decades:

> Picture a man … a man who has nowhere to go up the pyramid ladder in his local megachurch … a man who is rightly dressed up for the ministry but has nowhere to go. He starts a home study in his living room, hoping to find others who are ready for change. Like attracts like, and soon he manages to reel in other cheesed-off Christians who attract even more dissidents. In his own twisted and distorted lexicon he will call it biblical church planting, never realizing that he is about to enter into what his forbears have already discovered is in fact … the twilight zone.

Duh duh duh duh duh duh dum dumb!

This model has given church planting a bad name. Why do the eyes of so many pastors widen and twitch with fear at the mention of church planting? Planting that starts with Christians rather than non-believers strikes fear into the heart of any established pastor because it means that horse stealing is afoot—and that's a hanging offense in most churches!

The error, however, is on both sides of the divide. Shame on the church planter who is church planting simply because nobody will give him a church of his own! Perhaps if he keeps at it for ten years or so, he'll have a megachurch that resembles the one he left and be at the apex of his own pyramid. King of the Mountain is fun if you're at the top. Equal shame, however, is also due to the pastor who is afraid to lose people because he needs their money for fuel to keep the machine running.

The church is in the numbers business now, baby, and as Keith Green once said at Jesus NorthWest, "There is money to be made in Jesus's name!"[4]

FORMULAS FOR FAILURE

Remember the formula from earlier? Check it in reverse:

> *Formula 2:* Fewer people = less money = fewer toys = less ability to get people, which equals less money again.

The people are just a means to an end after all.

How have we let this happen to the church? How have we allowed this machine to grow into a giant Borg that desires to assimilate all species into the mothership for world domination? It's building your own personal empire versus building Christ's kingdom, and make no mistake, the world out there is watching. Church can become a pastor's own personal tower of Babel in which he refuses to spread out and multiply to the glory of God. Babel teaches us that bigger is not always better. You can tell the difference between empire builders and kingdom builders: personal empires build upward rather than outward. The kingdom, however, is not of this world and always builds outward. The size that it's concerned about is global, not local.

Why then is the current model all about keeping people in? And why does evangelism seem to be merely a way of *getting* people in so that we can *keep* them there? Ernest Hemingway may shed light on this. In *Green Hills of Africa*, Hemingway said that the writer only writes one pure book, and it's always his first. The first book is written out of his heart, as an expression of literary art. After his first book gets published, and he gains popularity, he becomes accustomed to a certain lifestyle. The need to keep this lifestyle going becomes a concern, and thereafter he writes to get published so that he can continue to maintain that higher standard of living. Many are beginning to feel this way about the ministry. When the success brings affluence and prestige, they leave the reckless abandon that caused them to go into the ministry in the first place. Once-daring pastors are waking up fifteen or twenty years later asking, "Is this what I signed up for?" They wanted to impact the world, serve Jesus, and grow in the process. But this isn't happening anymore.

Instead, pastors are reluctant to fulfill the Great Commission because their church would shrink, and with it their capacity to buy toys. Coming from a church that started out of the Jesus Movement, I've long rubbed shoulders with guys who saw miracles and witnessed the outpouring of the Holy Spirit upon a sex-crazed, drug-hazed generation. Years ago, my ex-hippie brother-in-law told me that there was a ceremony at a well-known Christian university where one of these ex-hippy pastors was asked to speak. He was known in the seventies as a countercultural, draft-card-burning, antiestablishment radical who'd do anything for Jesus, but his speech was a moralistic, right-wing diatribe that exhorted the students to "stay in school and get good grades" so they could be successful. My brother-in-law asked a friend standing nearby, "What happened to him?" The reply was, "He got rich." It explains a lot.

We have more now, which means that we have more to lose if we invest it in kingdom expansion.

Formula 3: Having more = having more to lose.

Once upon a time, a Franciscan monk visited Vatican City with a gift for the church. The pope took him on a personal tour, displaying the vast wealth of the Catholic Church. "Never again will the church be able to say, 'Silver and gold I do not have,'" he said. The Franciscan replied, "That may be true, but never again will the church be able to say, 'Rise up, take your mat, and walk.'"

The more we think kingdom expansion rather than empire building, the less we'll resemble CEOs and start looking like Neos; less businessmen, more radical revolutionaries; less pleasing to flesh, more threat to the Enemy. Are you ready to change things? Then *you've* got to be ready to change. And if you're ready to change, then the church is going to change. It's time for judgment to begin with the house of God. When we get it right, they'll get it right.

When I was trying to fit into a traditional pastorate like a square peg in a round hole, I came across an article in the Ikea catalog that profiled twenty-eight-year-olds. The article said this was the age when a man was most likely to disappear, change his name, leave his family, and drop off the face of the earth without a trace. Radiohead wrote a song about it: "How to Disappear Completely."[5] The article clawed fishhooks into my soul. I was twenty-eight years old, and I hated the ministry. My church sucked—but that's another story.

I would guess that many pastors are feeling the same way, but not because they shouldn't be in the ministry. They are called, but the church only has one caliber of bullet when it fires a man out of the barrel. Some of these guys who are church planting are biblical apostles (or missionaries) and, like Indiana Jones, were never meant to be Princeton lecturers. They were born to be temple-raiding adventurers. But they've been told they have to be pastors to serve God full-time. They've been tamed, castrated, stripped of their ability to fly.

These guys either discover who they really are, and like Neo get freed from the Matrix, or they claw at the walls until they burn out, sabotage themselves, or get fired. Every once in a while one of them wakes up and begins to see the Matrix code behind the illusion. Then it's kung-fu-kicking-butt-in-the-subway-time.

So before you turn the page, let me ask you: do you really want to take the red pill? It could cost you more than you're willing to lose.

And I warn ya, it's gonna hurt like heaven!

THE SECRET CLUB

*For it seems to me that God has put us apostles
on display … [as] the scum of the earth.*

Paul, 1 Corinthians 4:9, 13 NIV

*Give me one hundred preachers who fear nothing but sin
and desire nothing but God, and I care not a straw whether
they be clergymen or laymen; such alone will shake the gates
of hell and set up the kingdom of heaven on earth.*

John Wesley

*Men wanted for hazardous journey. Small wages, bitter
cold, long months of complete darkness, constant danger, safe
return doubtful. Honor and recognition in case of success.*

Ernest Shackleton, from the advertisement he used when
recruiting men for his expedition to Antarctica in 1914

Fred … you knew the job was dangerous when you took it!

Super Chicken

THE MASTER PLAN FROM THE MASTER OF THE UNIVERSE

When I was eight years old, He-Man was the Master of the Universe—well, of mine anyways. He held me spellbound in Eternia for half an hour every day. After the evil forces of Skeletor had been defeated, I found myself hungry for more eighties cheese and unwilling to wait until 23.5 hours elapsed.

So I watched She-Ra.

True, she may have been a girl, but she *was* the princess of power. She, too, hailed from Eternia, held aloft a magic sword by the power of Grayskull, kicked Skeletor sacrum,[1] and filled the next half-hour block. She was the next best thing after He-Man (besides Voltron), but she also boasted a feature that He-Man (as cool as he was) didn't have. She-Ra had Loo-Kee.

At the end of every show, a rainbow-colored smurf guy in overalls would pop out of a hole somewhere shouting, "Hi! I'm Loo-Kee—did you find me?" Usually I hadn't, because I'd been biting my pillow over the Evil Horde's seemingly undefeatable master plan. So Loo-Kee would help us out. He'd go back to the place in the show where you were supposed to notice him hiding behind some moss, or lurking in the shadows of a giant mushroom, and jump out. "Here I am!" he'd giggle, and we'd all feel stupid.

Crazy stuff, the eighties, but Loo-Kee wasn't so hard to find if only I kept my eyes open.

Do you know how many times I've heard people say, "I can't find the words *church planter* in the Bible"? It's there all right, but like finding Loo-Kee, you gotta keep your eyes peeled.

Apostle is the New Testament word for a pioneering, ground-breaking, foundation-laying, community-founding, team-building, mobile-discipling, self-replacing, church-planting missionary.

I don't know how many times I had read the book of Acts and Paul's epistles, hoping to get some angle on how the apostles got an edge over the pagan world that engulfed them, but I'd been ignoring the obvious the whole time. The role of the apostle as a church planter popped up all over the place in the New Testament, and I'd missed it. If you go back and watch the rerun of Acts, you'll see apostles as church planters jumping out from behind the narratives and shouting, "Did you find me? Here I am!" The true Master of the Universe *did* give us a master plan, but if we think we're smarter than Jesus, that mistake will eventually leave us feeling stupid.

The first thing the first-century church had was a working understanding of the role of an apostle. And that made all the difference.

BUT I CAN'T FIND "CHURCH PLANTER" IN MY BIBLE

C. Peter Wagner's now immortalized assertion that "the single most effective evangelistic methodology under heaven is planting new churches"[2] is not based solely on research, but also on the Acts of the Apostles. It's called the Acts of the *Apostles*, after all, but what *acts* are we supposed to notice? At the outset of Acts, their mind-set was simply to stay put, and NOT DO ANYTHING!

"Lord, will You at this time restore the kingdom?" was really the apostles' way of saying, "Jesus, this resurrection thing is great! *Can't we just have heaven on earth now?*"

Jesus told them that the schedule for kingdom restoration was none of their business—but then He said they were about to experience the power of the Holy Spirit that would fling them to the far corners of the earth to be His witnesses. The church's business isn't kingdom *restoration* but kingdom *expansion*, baby!

And how does the kingdom expand, according to the rest of the book?

Clear out some room, because I'm going to drop the A-bomb. When I drop this baby, apostolic shrapnel embeds itself through every square inch of the book of Acts.

Acts kicks off by recalling the founding of the world's first megachurch in Jerusalem as a church-planting hub. Because Acts is a book about church planting, it pitches Jerusalem as the church-planting base of operations. Luke was basically saying, "Now let me tell you about church planting in this region. This is how we did it.…" The structural narrative of Acts sticks to Jesus's words like Fat Albert on an ice cream truck: "you will be my witnesses in Jerusalem and in all Judea and Samaria, and to the end of the earth" (Acts 1:8). The emphasis is outward expansion—not just westward expansion, but eastward, northward, and southward—through apostolic church planting. The train of Luke's narrative leaves the platform at Jerusalem Grand Central Station, making its first scheduled church-planting stops in Judea, Samaria, and finally Antioch in Asia Minor. It all goes down just like Jesus said it would.

No surprises.

Then the rest of Paul's journeys were chronicled as he moved north by northwest, planting churches throughout Asia Minor until he finally reached Rome, the heart of the omni-powerful empire. Each station platform in Acts 13–21 was another church plant, until the whistle blew and Paul boarded the train to the next sovereignly appointed stop on his three missionary journeys. The Acts of the Apostles could be entitled the Acts of the Church Planters, and Paul's lesser apostles were essential to the kingdom's expansion on earth.

Wait a second....

If the role of apostles is essential to kingdom expansion, then why have we pretended for the last 1700 years that the office doesn't exist anymore? Why do I say 1700 years? Because the apostolic role of church planting was up and running for the first three hundred years of the church. The apostolic church-planting role continued beyond Paul's execution well into the second century. Eusebius said that during the second century, apostolic activity continued: "There were still many evangelists of the Word eager to use their inspired zeal *after the example of the apostles* for the increase and building up of the divine Word."[3] He added that "after laying the foundation of the faith in foreign parts as the particular object of their mission, and after appointing others as shepherds of ... those who had been recently introduced [to the faith] ... *they went again to other regions and nations*."[4] These guys were mobile.

The pattern continued from Paul to Timothy and others and into the second century. After that we lose the trail a bit. Do you know why? For two reasons. First, in the third century the church experienced "the Great Persecution," which led to fragmented accounts and scattered saints. The second reason is related to something my high school history teacher Mr. Osborn used to say: "The winner rewrites history." Eusebius was writing about church planters who continued to function like the apostles, but he had to call them evangelists because his fourth-century theology didn't allow anything else. The church has had a nasty historical habit of calling her apostolic offspring by safer names, such as pastors or missionaries.

However, whether you call them apostles or not, if they're serial church planters, they're apostles. Some of my church-planting friends are clearly apostles in the vein of Timothy and Titus, but their theology of apostolic expiration doesn't allow them to call themselves that. Nonetheless, a rose by any other name would smell as sweet. Functionally there were apostles "after the examples of the apostles," and then something happened in the fourth century that put a stop to all of that.

One word: Constantine.

THE COVER-UP

In 312 Emperor Constantine converted to Christ after a decisive battle. He waved a magic wand over the Roman Empire, legalizing Christianity and starting the church down the dark path of institutionalism. Being sucked into Rome seemed a whole heck of a lot better for Christians than becoming ground sausage for zoo animals in an amphitheater. Yet history has demonstrated that the church as an institution loses more than she gains. A church that is bought becomes a church that is sold. What did we sell under Constantine?

When Christianity was legalized in the Empire, it lost its evangelistic edge. Constantine's missionary philosophy was simple: "convert or die." It was pretty effective. The patriarchs waved the holy "okay" sign over the Empire, and all were "Christianized" with such success that the office of apostle became obsolete. Apostolic church planters were replaced with bishops and other ecclesiastical hierarchy that, to this day, wear very tall hats. Kiss kingdom expansion good night.

That's not to say that apostles weren't still operating. Like apostles today, they obeyed the call to expand the kingdom through church planting, but on the whole it was often in the face of the establishment. Patrick, the fifth-century apostle to the Irish, trained up converts who later trained and turned Columba, Aidan, and others loose on the world in the sixth and seventh centuries. Augustine of Canterbury evangelized the Saxons in Britain beginning in 597, and the Saxons then sent missionaries back to Germany to evangelize their Rome-resistant kin. Cyril and Methodius embarked on missions to Bulgaria in the ninth century and became known as the "Apostles to the Slavs." The Holy Spirit wasn't inactive; He kept the apostolic expansion alive as a sometimes-underground movement.

The church eventually called the pre-Constantine years the Apostolic and Post-Apostolic Age, as if the office was a relic of the past, and spoke of a time when giants roamed the earth. But what if I told you that the church was beginning to unearth the long-buried doctrine of biblical apostolic teams? It'd be like unearthing the ark of the covenant. It wouldn't decimate Nazi hordes or melt people's faces off, but it would put rocket fuel in the tank of kingdom expansion!

WHY'D IT HAVE TO BE SNAKES?

The Well of Souls in *Raiders of the Lost Ark* was a pit nobody wanted to venture down into. Standing on that sandy plateau of desert rocks, Indiana Jones was determined to lift that slab and raise the lost secret weapon of the kingdom of God. Lightning and thunder were sufficient omens for local Arab diggers to break and run at this point in the movie, and throwing down the torch on the word *apostle* makes most evangelicals similarly edgy. They say, "Son, you just leave that slab there, buried under the sand." Sorry, but no can do. Like Indy, we've got to keep digging.

There are three reasons for the fear of the office of apostle as church planter. First of all, something like the ark of the covenant that has been buried for ages accumulates massive quantities of dust and cobwebs. Dust is the obscurity that settles over a truth with time. When Martin Luther unearthed justification by faith again, it had been so buried that it was considered a radical church-splitting doctrine! But it was true. Have we become so arrogant that we honestly believe there are no more doctrines that have become obscured by our traditions? *Sola fide* had largely lain dormant until the 1500s![5]

Secondly, that dark hole is filled with a nest of snakes waiting to sink their fangs into anybody who disturbs the resting place of this doctrine. Let's face it: talking about apostleship in polite company at any pastor party is a way to ensure not getting invited back. It gets you labeled as the kid who smells.

But lastly, and perhaps most important, is that we genuinely fear that we're touching something that God buried long ago, and that by raising it up with pulleys and ropes we'll be acting against

His will, inadvertently invoking divine wrath. But what if man had buried it?

I want to address all three of these valid fears in this chapter, but first we need to look at what's at stake if we refuse to heed the Scripture.

Indy had it easy. If he didn't get to the ark first, the Nazis would. But we've got bigger fish to fry. We've got the entire world machine marching into hell, and the church is in retreat. I'm afraid I'm just going to have to ride this jackal statue through the wall here and come out swinging because, to put it frankly, there's no other way out of this pit.

Our reluctance to use the word *apostle* is primarily due to a misunderstanding of what an apostle is. The cobwebs of freaky teaching need to be brushed aside, and the dust of traditionalism needs to be blown off so that we can get a good look at it under the torchlight of Scripture. As for the snakes ready to attack, there was a time when I would have groaned, "Snakes. Why did it have to be snakes?" But where I've been crusading the last few years, church planting kills your reputation faster than anything. As a preacher once said, "God can't really use a man unless he's first killed his reputation." There goes what little was left of mine....

THE SCREAMING POTATOES

Before I became too cool to be in the Boy Scouts anymore, we used to camp every month. Each troop was broken down into groups of ten to twelve scouts called patrols. Each patrol had a unique name. Ours was called the Screaming Potatoes, and our patrol's chow box had a painting of a potato screaming as it sailed through the air. We got this name because somebody in our patrol (cough) decided that rather than cooking the tubers, we should lob them at the other patrols under the cover of night while they innocently cooked their Dutch-oven campfire meals.

Let's start by looking at the two major views on apostleship out there today as if they were separate patrols. Basically, there are two major camps, each huddling around a campfire and chucking hard potatoes at those huddled around the other. My hope is that we can gather up all of their abused taters off the ground and go make our own camp. And we know that potatoes are better mashed than thrown.

Besides, we have to think of the tots.

CAMP 1: THE SECRET CLUB

Next time you're standing in line for the Pirates of the Caribbean ride under the hot California sun at Disneyland, look over to the top of the Blue Bayou restaurant. Ever wondered what's up there?[6] Well, it ain't the Mickey Mouse Club. Disneyland has an elite Dinner Club called Club 33. Originally, it was a place where Walt Disney wanted movie stars and dignitaries to be treated like royalty while they were his personal guests in the park, but he died before it was finished. You probably didn't even know it was there. That's because you're not meant to, unless you've endured the eleven-year waiting list and paid ten thousand clams to be a card-carrying Club member. Nobody knows why it was called Club 33, but one theory is that there were thirty-three initial members/investors when Disney first pitched it.

Likewise, Jesus had many followers who trailed Him like the crowds at Disneyland trying to meet Mickey, but He, too, had an elite club exclusively made up of twelve disciples. We'll call it Club 12.

Let's see what the first camp is doing with their potatoes.

Camp 1 is called the Secret Club. There are variations within this camp, but they agree that the role of apostle didn't survive the first century after the canon of Scripture was complete. They also believe that Matthias was mistakenly chosen to take Judas's place instead of Paul. They have to affirm this because they say that there were only twelve chosen apostles, and to acknowledge lesser apostles would undermine their fixed belief that there were only twelve directly appointed by Jesus. They say Paul snuck into Club 12 through the kitchen entrance a little late, but he should have been chosen to replace Judas the traitor. They believe that the apostles rolled the dice too soon. Matthias would have gotten away with it too, if it hadn't been for those meddling kids later unmasking Paul as the true replacement.

Let's chuck some potatoes at them.

Chucking Potatoes at the Secret Club

First screaming potato: I can see why people would think Paul was the true replacement, except for the fact that Acts 6:2 says "*the twelve* summoned the full number of disciples." Luke wrote those words knowing that Matthias was one of those twelve when Paul wasn't even saved yet. If Luke in Acts 6:2 didn't have a problem identifying Matthias as one of the Twelve, then why do we?

But they say, "We never hear of Matthias again in the book of Acts." If that's the case, then we'd better kiss off Andrew, Thomas, Bartholomew, James son of Alpheus, and Simon the Zealot as members of the original Club 12, because after Acts 1:13 they're never mentioned again either.

The truth is, Paul never considered himself a card-carrying member of the exclusive Club 12, so neither should we. Paul did consider himself to be equal to the Twelve in authority, abilities, and qualifications, yet not one of their number. In other words, he didn't redub the apostolic posse as Club 13. Why then was it important that he be seen as their equal in qualifications and authority?

Paul's credentials of apostleship were frequently under fire. In Galatia, the Judaizers claimed he wasn't a real apostle because he wasn't one of the Twelve. In Corinth, false teachers or "super-apostles" (2 Cor. 11:5, 13) claimed that they themselves were superior to Paul. In Acts, Luke validated Paul's ministry as an apostle to the Gentiles in the second part of his book, just as he validated the Twelve as the apostles to the twelve tribes of Israel in the first part of his book.[7] Stephen's martyrdom in Acts 7 signals Israel's final rejection of the gospel, and from chapter 9 onward Luke switched tracks in his narrative, primarily following Paul as the apostle to the Gentiles and establishing that his ministry was on equal footing.[8] Luke did this for the next twenty chapters, giving the lion's share of attention to Paul's ministry to the Gentiles.

Because Acts hadn't been written yet, the Corinthians hadn't gotten the memo. So the false teacher "super-apostles" claimed that Paul was like Bruce Wayne with no superpowers—like superior public-speaking abilities or heat-ray vision—and therefore couldn't play pool with the Justice League. Because of these claims, the credentials of Club 12 apostleship are a big topic in 1 Corinthians. Here's the curriculum vitae of an apostle with Club 12 status:

1. *You had to have seen the risen Lord.* Peter said, "One of these men must become with us a witness of his resurrection" (Acts 1:22), and the church appointed Matthias. Paul said he wasn't inferior to the Twelve in this regard because he encountered the risen Christ on the road to Damascus (1 Cor. 9:1). That meeting was credential enough to validate his apostleship to the Gentiles.

2. *You had to be there from the beginning.* Luke quoted Peter as saying that Judas's replacement had to be somebody who "accompanied us during all the time that the Lord Jesus went in and out among us, beginning from the baptism of John until the day when he was taken up from us" (Acts 1:21–22). Paul seemed aware of the requirement when he said he was "born out of due time" (1 Cor. 15:8 NKJV). Paul wasn't there from the beginning, but in his mind, two out of three wasn't bad. When Jesus appears to you and commissions you as an apostle, you get a divine hall pass on this one. Nobody would have denied Paul's apostleship on this front, except maybe Internet trolls, but they didn't exist in the first century.

Because of his meeting with the resurrected Jesus, Paul said he was equal to the Twelve. Yet nowhere did he say that the same qualifications applied to those he trained up after him, such as Timothy, Titus, and the others. So although witnessing the resurrection was necessary to be one of the Twelve, it was not necessary to be an apostle to the Gentiles. We know this because Timothy, Apollos, and the others were all called *apostolos*, yet they never saw the risen Lord Jesus. There was a distinction between the Twelve—the greater apostles to the twelve tribes—and Paul's lesser apostles. We're talking Apostles with a capital A versus apostles with a little "a." Paul himself appears to be a linchpin hybrid between the two. Paul was the 13th Warrior added to the twelve, but with a difference. He was born out of due time because he wasn't meant to be an apostle to the Jews. No, he was the apostle to the Gentiles. The Jews had twelve for each tribe; the Gentiles had Paul. And Paul had at least thirty-two guys he reproduced himself into.

3. *You had to do miracles.* Not the Father Guido Sarducci variety, but power-of-God stuff. Paul reminded the Corinthians that he did miracles like those in Club 12, who were said to be "true apostles," as a sign among them (2 Cor. 12:12).

Therefore, Paul ranks himself equal to the Twelve, but not a member of Club 12 itself.

Not to muddy the argument, but there also seemed to have been "lesser apostles" in the Jerusalem camp too. In Paul's postresurrection appearance chronology, he mentioned that Jesus appeared to "the twelve" (1 Cor. 15:5), and then "to all the apostles" (1 Cor. 15:7). Who are the rest of the apostles? We don't know for sure, but it's fair to speculate that Barnabas was one of them, as the word *apostolos* is used for him as well (Acts 14:14).

Third screaming potato: there are some in the Secret Club who will cry uncle if put into a scriptural full nelson and who will allow that Timothy, Titus, and others in Paul's posse could be dubbed apostles. But, they say, when the canon of Scripture was completed, that office faded away like an old soldier. If we have the epistles, who needs apostles? They also argue that the church is built upon the foundation of the apostles and prophets. They have a point. After all, you can only lay a foundation once, so it seems that the apostles were laid down once and for all. They reason this from 1 Corinthians 13:8–10, which says:

> Love never ends. As for prophecies, they will pass away; as for tongues, they will cease; as for knowledge, it will pass away. For we know in part and we prophesy in part, but when the perfect comes, the partial will pass away.

The idea is that when "the perfect" comes, prophesies, knowledge, and tongues (and, we're meant to assume, apostles) will cease. But what does "the perfect" in that passage mean? Last time I checked, the perfect referred to the return of Christ at the dawn of the eternal age, not the completion of the canon during the first century. Paul was saying that love will continue into eternity. There will be no need for hope, because hope will be realized in eternity. Faith will not be required, because we will have sight when Jesus comes. Love, however—love is eternal.

Yet Scripture never even breathes a hint that the office of apostle is going to stop before that day. They are right about one thing regarding apostleship in that passage. When Jesus returns, there'll be no more use for that role, and I'll be out of a job. Woohoo! I've needed a vacation.

Therefore, if we're looking for scriptural reasons why the role of apostle isn't for today, I'm afraid you just witnessed the shattering of the best argument against it. As Rocky Balboa would say, "Is that all you got?"

Before moving on to the next camp, I emphasize that holding the view of present-day lesser apostles doesn't open the door for people to write new books of the Bible at Starbucks this afternoon. In the first place, the Twelve didn't write much Scripture. Only Matthew, John, and Peter did. The lion's share of the New Testament easily goes to Paul and Luke, not to mention Jude, James, Mark, and the mystery man who wrote Hebrews. The canon of Scripture *has been completed*, but that's inferred through history and Jude 1:3, that the faith was "once for all delivered to the saints," not from 1 Corinthians 13. When the apostle John died, forever closed the eyes that had witnessed Jesus's entire ministry from John's baptism to his ascension (Acts 1:22), and the age of inspired writing of Scripture also breathed its last.

That oughta make everybody breathe easier.

Spotting Elvis

Question: What do Elvis and the Apostles have in common?

Punch line: Everybody knows they are dead, but that doesn't stop people from claiming to have seen them walking around in local supermarkets.

So let's recap. Apostles with a big A are the Twelve. Never to be repeated, these guys founded the Jerusalem church. Apostles with a little "a" are church planters, and they're wired for church expansion. Always to be repeated, these guys carry kingdom expansion throughout the ages by means of planting churches. Without these guys, the church will continue to hobble along at a snail's pace as it attempts to eke out a convert here and there.

Therefore, if you think you see Elvis out there running around, no matter how much it looks like the King, it's an Elvis impersonator. As a church planter, I consider myself an Elvis impersonator. I am imitating my Master, I'm imitating the Apostles, but I myself am not special. I could probably get a gig in Vegas, but it'd be at a small club, because there are thousands just like me. We have no superpowers, have not seen the risen Lord, and pretty much just plant churches.

Theologian Wayne Grudem helpfully allowed for this view when he said, "Today some people use the word apostle in a very broad sense, to refer to an effective church planter, or to a significant missionary pioneer.... If we use the word apostle in this broad sense, everyone would agree that there are still apostles today."[9]

CAMP 2: CLUB INFINITY

This brings us to the camp on the other side of the potato-chucking no-man's-land. We'll call them Club Infinity on account of them having an indefinite membership open to any number of Apostles with big As. If only church history weren't littered with these guys claiming to be "super-apostles" (2 Cor. 11:5; 12:1). These guys are guilty of so many abuses that it's made most people avoid the word *apostle* altogether. This club doesn't believe in Elvis impersonators; they believe that an apostle is the king. Hunk a hunk o' burning authority. Like Uncle Ben said to Spidey, "With Big A comes great authority," and the guys at Club Infinity believe that there are guys of John's, Peter's, and James's status walking around today.

Meanwhile, back at Club 33 ...

In the early days of Disneyland's Club 33, only rich investors, movie stars, famous musicians, and important dignitaries ever saw the interior of the lobby. When you enter the lobby of Club 33, it appears as if you've stepped through a time warp into the French Quarter of New Orleans circa nineteenth century. You stand before a gilded glass elevator that you swore Willy Wonka and Charlie Bucket took a joyride in. How do I know?

I've ridden in it.

I'm not rich, nor am I extremely patient. So I didn't wait eleven years or pay ten grand. Instead, a connected church-planter friend hooked me up with a dinner reservation. It meant that I got the rare experience of pressing the secret doorbell in the secret cubbyhole and saying, "Jones, party of five," over the secret intercom. Then the moment arrived. The door cracked open, and a Disney employee with all of the mystique of an Oompa Loompa opened the door and ushered my party inside.

You wanna know what I thought when I got in there? *Neat ... but they must have lowered the standards if they let rabble like me in on somebody else's ticket.*

And lowered it they had. Over the years, the invite to Club 33 went from being reserved for a select few to being broadened to include those who had eleven years to kill and ten thousand bucks to burn. By doing so, it lost some of its exclusivity. Likewise the second camp on apostleship has broadened Club 12 by issuing more A Apostle elite membership cards and extending access to the elite club that Jesus set up. Let me tell you why we should throw potatoes at them.

It's the big A that makes me edgy. Club Infinity believes that there are super apostles still walking around. What is a super apostle? You don't want to meet one. These guys supposedly know all of your secrets, are rumored to burn holes into your soul with their eye-bullets, and can inexplicably make your armpits stink and sweat when you're in secret sin just by looking in your general direction. No wonder no one wants these guys around. I just don't buy it. To make matters worse, these guys usually wield Castle Grayskull amounts of power, and people do whatever they say. On the ground, these guys have metaphorical pontifical cigar-shaped rocket hats decreeing rules like whether all women should or should not wear hats to church. And because they have pope-like status, they should never ever be questioned.

I smell potential for abuse.

Unfortunately, this is how the term *apostle* has been misused and abused by people who want to keep others under their thumbs. Even Paul didn't mosey, swagger, brag, or brawl like he was the John Wayne of Christendom. He was a humble guy who exalted lowliness. He confessed that he wasn't very slick, admitting that his speaking ability kinda sucked. He probably didn't wear a white suit, have big hair, or get all of the chicks like most TV preachers. He hadn't even attained the rock-star status of super apostle in the eyes of the churches he planted (2 Cor. 11:5) and confessed he never lorded authority over people (1:24).

Nobody treated him like a five-star general. Hierarchy was foreign to him because his ministry operated out of respect. The young men and women in his sphere respected and served him because they knew nobody else had suffered as much for the gospel as he had. Nonetheless, he never deemed the younger apostles to be less than himself by calling them "delegates" or "apprentices"; instead he called them "partners with me in the work" and "fellow workers." He did not demand obedience to his personal wishes. He said, "Now concerning our brother Apollos, I strongly urged him to visit you with the other brothers, but it was not at all his will to come now. He will come when he has opportunity" (1 Cor. 16:12). Did you catch that? You could tell Paul no, and he'd still work with you. Unbelievable.

In my travels over the years I've accidentally met a couple of these self-appointed A-postles, and to be honest, the only thing worthy of a capital A was their arrogance. I'd probably be arrogant too if somebody treated me like I was equal to the apostle John and treated my words like Scripture. Seriously, within sixty seconds of being let into Club 33 I spilled half a wheel of Corner Bakery coffee cake all over the floor of the lobby as I folded up my baby's stroller. I'm not lying. I think I made Disneyland history. If I made that kind of mess after they let me into their elite club, I can only imagine the mess these super Apostle guys make with people's lives. The fact is, the Club never should have been this big. It was made to hold only twelve people. It was special, and the door to membership was closed long ago.

If the term *apostle* is merely the New Testament word for *missionary*, then what does that mean about the missionaries you know? Chances are, you wouldn't want to swap lives with them for any price. When they come home, they're still wearing Bermuda shorts and don't know what TiVo and iPods are. Nonetheless, because a guy's a missionary, he's the one always looking outward while the pastor is looking inward. Don't let those Bermudas fool you; he's God's dangerous secret weapon. You might snicker at his fashion sense, but demons are trembling when he gets back on the plane to do what God's called him to.

In the West we're in desperate need of more of these guys on our church leadership teams so that we can regain the missionary edge that was lost after the fourth century. This edge was sharpened again during the whetstone of the Reformation, the Great Awakening, and any time that the church needed to be propelled out of a rut.

Just like now.

And whenever you find that sharpening in church history, and the church has regained its edge, you'll find an apostle in the eye of the hurricane.

Evan Roberts, Charles Spurgeon, David Martyn Lloyd-Jones, Whitefield, Wesley, and others time would fail me to tell of …

The Brave, the Poor, the Church Planter

Although church planting may sound sexy, it's not. At our first conference we handed the guys in New Breed a rock and told them that this was what church planting was like. It was hard, small, and inglorious. The funny thing is that if Paul put an ad in the paper of what it meant to be an apostle, most men in pastoral ministry wouldn't answer it. Here's Paul's description of apostles/church planters in the first century:

> For I think that God has exhibited us apostles as last of all, like men sentenced to death, because we have become a spectacle to the world, to angels, and to men. We are fools for Christ's sake, but you are wise in Christ. We are weak, but you are strong. You are held in honor, but we in disrepute. To the present hour we hunger and thirst, we are poorly dressed and buffeted and homeless, and we labor, working with our own hands. When reviled, we bless; when persecuted, we endure; when slandered, we entreat. We have become, and are still, like the scum of the world, the refuse of all things. (1 Cor. 4:9–13)

It's a fact. Church planters are usually unpopular, underpaid, and under attack while planting churches. They don't bring in the huge numbers and often wouldn't be considered "successful" by today's ministry standards. Success is seen as building upward, but their job is to spread the church outward. Like their first-century counterparts, apostles/church planters don't stay still for long to be studied under a microscope. When Dr. Luke decided to assess them, he had to do it on the road, so he became a participant in Paul's journeys like a rock journalist going on tour with the band. Those who traveled with Paul didn't last long because they lacked the endurance for the chilled nights, the starving hours, and the miles traveled.

Apostolos in Paul's day was understood literally as a "messenger" and referred to a traveling courier whose sole mission was to deliver the message at all costs. Like a rider in the Pony Express, he was often in danger of being mugged, beaten, or killed. Often destitute of food and clothes, he was a marked man. Nonetheless, he accepted his message with determination, regardless of cost, oblivious to personal consequence. It was a dangerous job many didn't want. It's understandable why Paul used it to describe his own role after he was attacked by wild beasts, beaten, stoned, whipped, and shipwrecked.

Dangerous People

I went to seminary. It was a great experience, and I learned loads of stuff about exposition. I'd gladly do it again, but when you pay thousands of dollars to a seminary, you exit the building with only a diploma, some neat knowledge in your noggin, and maybe the ability to preach. Certain seminaries will throw in counseling as a bonus. The question that's been boggling my bowl for years is why the curriculum can be so heavy, take so long, cost so much, and yet never teach our boys how do anything like what you find in the book of Acts. These brain-heavy, pasty-white, book-nosed seminarians are more wired for holding ground than taking it. That's criminal. It's like joining the 101st Airborne, going to jump school, and graduating never having jumped out of an airplane!

The guys that we tend to write books about were guys who knew how to strap on the parachute, yell "Geronimo!" and free fall into no-man's-land to take new ground.

Apostles often appear reckless to respectable church folks. They are in good company, however. Most of the people heralded in the halls of faith in Hebrews 11 or the annals of church history were dangerous, unpredictable, and downright embarrassing to have around at times. Most of the churches who laud their heroics wouldn't touch these guys with a ten-foot pole if they were looking for a pastor. Like the Pharisees, we build monuments to their memories, but we'd probably have stoned them if they lived in our era. But if we mount the bleachers of church history and observe those who ran before us, whizzing by are athletes who didn't fit the pastor mold and didn't necessarily fit the straitjacketed evangelist moniker either.

They were something else.

When these guys went places, stuff happened. Things changed. Communities came alive. Movements started. Tidal waves swept nations. They were catalysts. They were apostles.

They were church planters, and they changed the world. That's what dangerous people do. Today it's trendy in church-planting circles to call them "entrepreneurial leaders" instead of apostles. Whatever—history is filled with them.

Take William Carey. He doesn't seem too dangerous at first glance. A shoe cobbler by trade, part-time teacher by occupation. He hammered the soles of shoes absentmindedly while gazing up at the map on his wall, allowing his mind to wander into a recurring day-dream that one day he would sail to foreign lands to bring the hope of the cross to exotic peoples. He launched out in the days where you shipped your possessions in a six-foot pine box, because most likely that's how you were coming home: in a coffin. Embarking to India, he translated the Scripture into numerous languages, leading scores to Christ, planting churches, and opening the floodgates for future missionaries. Not only that, he tirelessly reproduced himself in the native population to which he was called.

Hailed as the Father of Modern Missions, he wasn't just a pastor. What was he then? A gospel-pioneering missionary? Hmmm … kinda long and unwieldy for a title. I think I remember reading a Greek word for one of those somewhere in the New Testament. He was a church planter. He was an apostle.

Martin Luther. This guy started an underground countercultural movement of monks, nuns, and peasants who hefted the gospel throughout Germany, at dire risk to their lives, and founded new churches based upon the truths of the gospel. Strangely, he wasn't a full-time pastor. Think about it. A world-shaping, culture-changing, history-making catalyst, and yet we can't think what title to give his role in the kingdom of Christ?

I think Jesus had one.

From 1555 to 1562 John Calvin sent eighty-eight church plant-ers from Geneva into France. Some were successful; nine paid the ultimate price of martyrdom. When they started, there was only one Reformed church there. At the end of this period, however, there were 2150 Reformed churches that had been planted or replanted and were preaching the gospel.[10] If that's not apostolic kingdom expansion, then nothing is—yet Calvin struggled with what his eyes witnessed. He speculated that apostles may have been resurfacing during the Reformation, but he was unable to commit himself to using the term, believing that they existed only in the first century. Yet his eyes seemed to be playing tricks on him like tiny round devils. He wrote:

> Those … functions which were not instituted in the church to be perpetual, but only to endure so long as churches were to be formed where none previously existed … although I deny not, that afterward God occasionally raised up Apostles, or at least Evangelists, in their stead, as has been done in our time.[11]

Calvin, Luther, and others like them scanned the horizon, looking for the role of apostle without looking into the mirror to see that they themselves were the closest fits. In fact, every time God catalyzed the church out of a lull in missional expansion, He sent revolutionaries who rediscovered His heart and raised the banner on the wreckage of the church furniture. In the midst of those times, you'll find an apostle stirring things up. Like the students in *Les Miserables*, these renegades raged against the machine, yet were raised up to expand the kingdom on earth. Whitefield and Wesley weren't pastors for long but instigated worldwide spiritual revolutions that left church plants in every community they swept through. These men had wider ministries than just some local pastorate confined to four walls and a pulpit. George Whitefield once exclaimed, "All the world is my pulpit." So say biblical apostles with little a's.

A DANGEROUS BOOK

It's time for a revolution.

The red-letter, gold-leaf-edged, leather-bound fatty in your hand is a dangerous book. It has been changing people's minds for eons. It will obliterate your pretty little boxes, and not many people have the stomach for that. The Reformation should remind us that sometimes the truth is eccentric in its time, but Bertrand Russell once said, "Do not fear to be eccentric in opinion, for every opinion now accepted was once eccentric." It is time that the church recognizes this important role, recovers the biblical doctrine of church planting, and learns to call a spade a spade. Or in this case, a church planter an apostle.

Have you started to spot Loo-Kee in pages of the New Testament? If not, I hope you feel stupid.

3

THE A-TEAM

But I do not account my life of any value nor as precious to myself,
if only I may finish my course and the ministry that I received
from the Lord Jesus, to testify to the gospel of the grace of God.

Paul, Acts 20:24

I wish we had no circuit with fewer than three preachers on it, or less
than four hundred miles' riding in four weeks.... If we do not take
care, we shall all degenerate into milksops. "Soldiers of Christ, arise!"

John Wesley, *Letters*

If you have a problem, if no one else can help, and if you
can find them ... maybe you can hire the A-Team.

The A-Team, opening monologue

Float like a butterfly, sting like a bee!

Muhammad Ali

MUST ... REACH ... MY ... UTILITY BELT ...

There is an A-Team in the Bible. It's the team of interchangeable ministry specialists that Paul traveled with in the book of Acts. The church of Christ, minus the biblical understanding of the apostolic team (or A-Team), is like Batman minus his utility belt. What would he be without his smoke pellets, grappling hook, batarang, and bat-cuffs? Let's face it, the Dark Knight stripped down to his tights is really just a glorified ninja. Without his belt, Batman might as well be naked. Joker always strips him of it while dangling him over a vat of acid. Batman's always saved if he can "just reach it" within seconds of falling headlong. Utility belts are for utilizing, and Satan has been holding it away from us for so long, we've forgotten how to use our kit. The church is all tights, no batbelt.

Like the Caped Crusader, we don't have superpowers. Therefore we're gonna need all the kit supplies in our arsenal! We can't afford to pick our favorite tool. If Batman only used one tool from his utility belt, his movies, games, and comics would suck. The church has been limiting itself to only one tool for centuries: the pastor. But we can do so much more. Our utility belt has multiple compartments labeled *apostle*, *prophet*, *evangelist*, and *teacher*.

Don't get me wrong—Batman could still do the job without all of his tools. I mean, he *is* Batman after all, and he's much more than his belt. A glorified ninja is still a ninja (and a ninja'll cut your head off). The church is still the body of Christ, the most powerful spiritual ninja in the universe! We are a superhero empowered by Jesus to put the Devil's lights out. Even the gates of hell are incompetent to drive us back into extinction. But are we content with that? Content with not becoming totally extinct?

What about the forward movement Jesus talked about? Is it just me, or are we supposed to be driving back the darkness? When the church recovers all the tools in the utility belt, it's lights out for the Enemy, and lights on for the kingdom! Wouldn't it be great to get the Devil shaking his head in disbelief as we retake Gotham, muttering to himself like the Joker, "Where does the church get all those wonderful toys?"

MADE TO SPREAD

I want to challenge the next generation of church leaders to go back to New Testament principles that ensure a church's survival of any cultural revolution. I'm crying *sola scriptura* at the top of my lungs and challenging leaders to embody that spirit. Any church that fails to do so will soon become just another subculture that has failed to infiltrate its surrounding culture. Understanding the biblical A-Team is indispensable for a biblical church expansion.

What is this team's special mission? What ground is it supposed to take?

You may not view yourself as a church planter, but every church has a responsibility to spread the gospel beyond its own four walls. For far too long, churches have lied to themselves, saying that if they can just get people within their four walls, they've spread the gospel. The more people you cram inside, the more you can tell yourself you're spreading the gospel. But what about the people outside at the liquor stores and pool halls, on the bar stools, in the gay bars, released today from prison, loitering in the parks, eating out of garbage cans?

Simply put, we don't give a rip.

We're in the numbers game. I'd be rich if I had a dollar for every time I've seen a Christian leader playing turf wars like Al Capone. There are plenty of fish in the sea, but if we really cared about fishing, we'd have drawn the conclusion that the more nets in the water, the more fish turn up at the market. But we're not as interested in catching fish as in gaining profit. After all, we've got some big bills to pay. The lighting bill of many churches alone would cost more than you make in a year. Churches are in competition because when you've got a megachurch as your endgame, another church in the area is simply siphoning off the numbers of your accumulation and thinning your potential profit. That's okay though, because the other guy also wants to be the Highlander with immortal powers, and you know what immortals say: "There can be only one."

Paul had a different attitude. Paul knew that some were preaching Christ out of selfish ambition. Nonetheless, he said, "Christ is proclaimed, and in that I rejoice" (Phil. 1:18).

DISASTER ON THE FRONT LINES

On D-Day, the 101st Airborne parachuted into Normandy, dressed to kill. Because each soldier had about 150 pounds of gear on him when fully loaded up, some genius in the US army dreamed up the infamous "leg bag" concept. It would allow the airborne infantry to parachute with bags attached to their legs that wouldn't compete for valuable gear space with the parachute packs on their backs. The jumpers loaded up their bags with everything they could, including their weapons.

There was one problem. Because Operation Overlord was already working on an oversized budget, they sought to cut costs wherever they could. Some official somewhere made the decision to use a very cheap piece of cord to fasten the leg bag to the jumper's boot. The result: the combination of a heavy bag and a cheap cord meant that the cord snapped when the parachute opened, and the packs of guns, ammo, grenades, and rations were scattered in fields and bushes throughout the breadth of Normandy. This is why in the miniseries *Band of Brothers* Lieutenant Winters is seen wielding a knife in the dark rather than a Thompson rifle on his first night in France.

The other major fiasco was that the pilots flying the C-47 planes were meant to throttle down to ninety miles per hour in order to allow the paratroopers a safe landing. Due to low-lying clouds, German searchlights, tracers, and explosions, the pilots banked left, right, climbed or descended in altitude, and sped up to a hundred and fifty miles per hour to avoid being shelled. The result was that the paratroopers were jumping haphazardly, scattered over farmland, townships, rivers, and roads. One soldier even landed in a pile of manure. As Stephen Ambrose said, "At least it was a soft landing."[1]

This is the lesson: they didn't make any headway until they reassembled. It's going to be the same for us. We have been a scattered bunch of one-hit wonders, trying to be the next Spurgeon,

Lloyd-Jones, Piper, or Driscoll. If that's been your focus, I've got news for you, pal. It probably isn't going to happen. We're going to need to reassemble ourselves according to the roles Jesus assigned us and relocate our equipment if we're going to make headway in preventing the Great Commission from becoming the great omission.

We've become so scattered and out of formation that we're not even clear what our directives are anymore. David Garrison challenged:

> If we want to be on mission with God we simply must pause long enough to understand how God is on mission. Only then can we know with some degree of certainty that we are aligned as his instruments and not misaligned as his obstacles.[2]

How is God on mission? Jesus said, "As you have sent me into the world, so I have sent them into the world" (John 17:18), but are we going as He went?

Church planting is essentially bringing the unique gospel community presence of Jesus Christ (where two or more are gathered) into the midst of a surrounding non-gospel community: "I am there in the midst of them" (Matt. 18:20 NKJV). It is the process of transforming a city into a city on a hill by shining a beacon of God's glory in its midst. A scene in Peter Jackson's film *The Two Towers* depicts a relay of signal fires being lit across Middle Earth. The awesome responsibility of any church planter is to light the signal fires that stretch the breadth of the land, so that from any one point on the street-view of God's Google map, you have God's POV within a community.

Ambitious? Maybe. But Jesus thought we could do it—through a Spirit-empowered team effort. As the ultimate apostle, Jesus spearheaded the mission, making the jump from heaven to earth. When His assignment was accomplished, He commissioned His sub-officers to finish the mission, rigged Himself back up to heaven, and kicked down five separate kitbags to help them finish the job.

IN THE KITBAG

Ephesians 4 helps us collect and identify the equipment, outlining the labels on the kitbags:

> "When He ascended on high,
> He led captivity captive
> And gave gifts to men...."

> And He Himself gave some to be apostles, some prophets, some evangelists, and some pastors and teachers, for the equipping of the saints for the work of ministry. (Eph. 4:8, 11–12 NKJV)

- Kitbag 1: apostle
- Kitbag 2: prophet
- Kitbag 3: evangelist
- Kitbag 4: pastor
- Kitbag 5: teacher

Are we using all the kitbags or just the one labeled "pastor"?

Kitbags are what commandos wear in addition to their parachutes. They contain tools to get the wet-work done. Our commanding officer dropped these five kitbags to transform *Mission Impossible* to *Mission Possible*. Once the understanding that these five roles worked together to accomplish the mission was called the fivefold ministry, but with all the weird and dysfunctional baggage attached to the term, it's been abandoned. Alan Hirsch and Michael Frost reworked the title to "APEST" (an acronym for apostle, prophet, evangelist, shepherd, teacher). If that works for you, cool. But whatever you call it, the biblical principle of team planting is essential.

Personally, I like the term FIST. It doesn't have the number five in it, and it isn't an acronym, but it's wicked cool. Fists of Fury, the Man with the Iron Fist. It speaks of doing some damage to the enemy. We all have two fists. Hold one out and study it. All five of your fingers come together toward the center of your hand to clench into a powerful weapon to bust teeth loose. All five fingers are uniquely different. My index finger points at you, my middle finger tells you I'm angry, my ring finger tells you I'm committed to you until death, and my pinky might have something to say about my sexual orientation if I extend it while drinking tea. My opposable thumb? Well, that allows me to hold it all together to pack a punch. Each finger, completely unique and impressive on its own, but not individually threatening, comes together to become a haymaker! That's pretty boss! From here on out, I'll be referring to the coming together of these five leaders as a combined force as FIST leadership.

FISTS OF JESUS

When Jesus ascended with His work unfinished, He knew that no one person was going to be able to follow in His wake. The five kitbags each represent a specific skillset necessary for a church leadership team, like a sapper, sniper, commando, Navy SEAL, and heavy weapons expert. A church planter is never a splinter cell who acts alone, but the leader of a platoon of daredevil pathfinders. Church planting resembles a covert commando operation that travels covertly in small teams, creates an opening for other special teams, and gets the heck out of Dodge when the mission is accomplished.

Wimps need not apply.

Typically, church-planting teams have not been very specialized. If somebody plants a church, it's assumed that he must be a pastor. What about the other four roles? Imagine Navy SEALs outfitted in full scuba gear getting ready to jump out of an airplane. They just don't have the kit. Don't get me wrong, a pastor may be called to plant, but he's going to need to jump with an apostle. If a pastor isn't particularly gifted on the evangelistic side of things, he's going to need somebody on hand with the evangelism kitbag.

What good would it be if we were all Navy SEALs? I need a sapper. I'm gonna probably need a sniper as well. If you've seen Stallone's *The Expendables*, you'll know that the individuals in that team of elite mercenaries were recruited because of their special skills. So were you. When Jesus recruits leaders, He equips them like a Stallone, Statham, Li, Lundgren, Couture, Austin, Crews, Rourke, or Willis to assemble a super-team of highly specialized talents. We may be a Dirty Dozen crew of specialized ex-convicts, but we have skills. *The Dirty Dozen* impacted cinematic history because it concentrated on special teams. If it had been called *The Dirty One*, it would have conveyed an entirely different meaning, or it would have blown as a film.

Nobody wants to watch one guy doing everything. Nobody buys it, and it doesn't work in real life. Because the church has assumed that all you need for simple shake-and-bake church planting is a pastor, the church has not learned to knit bands of special teams together, and rather than becoming the Expendables, they've often become the Disposables in terms of expanding the kingdom.

The church desperately needs to see the return of the A-Team.

The pastor-only club is killing the leadership of the church. Guys are burning out, losing their families, sabotaging their marriages, or simply going back to selling used cars. It's time those of you in ministry got your life back.

JESUS WAS AN ARMY OF ONE ... YOU'RE NOT

There was only one guy who could shoulder all five jobs on His own, and He's not physically camping out here anymore. Jesus was the Master Chief of those five roles. Master Chief is a cybernetic super-soldier who can use any weapon of any make, alien or otherwise, simply by picking it up. He possesses integrative software hardwired into his cyber-suit that immediately breaks down the operational component of any weapons system. You and I, unfortunately, do not possess such a suit. We're grunts. Therefore, we specialize.

A shepherd can't concentrate on evangelism; a teacher has to hit the books and resist being bogged down with too many namby-pamby counseling sessions. Jesus alone mastered all five roles:

- Apostle: "Consider Jesus, the apostle" (Heb. 3:1). Let's face it, He is the ultimate pioneer, missionary, messenger, and sent one.
- Prophet: "The LORD your God will raise up for you a prophet like me from among you, from your brothers—it is to him you shall listen" (Deut. 18:15). After Jesus gave the people bread in the wilderness like Moses did, John did the math for us: "When the people saw the sign that he had done, they said, 'This is indeed the Prophet who is to come into the world!'" (John 6:14). Good guess.
- Evangelist: When Jesus took the scroll in the synagogue at Nazareth, He read Isaiah 61:1, which says that He was anointed to "bring good news [gospel] to the poor" as well as liberty and the Lord's favor. If John's gospel presents Jesus as anything in His conversations, it presents Him as an evangelist.
- Shepherd: "I am the good shepherd" (John 10:11). Peter calls him our "chief Shepherd" (1 Peter 5:4).
- Teacher: "And he opened his mouth and taught them" (Matt. 5:2). "Never man spake like this man" (John 7:46 KJV). 'Nuff said.

FIST leadership isn't something we've made up; it's what our Master Chief has distributed to the church so that He can "fill all things" (Eph. 4:10). That means to spread out! Therefore, He calls some to be apostles, some evangelists ... you get the picture. Facing a task unfinished, we seek to fill the hole that He's left behind.

When Bugs Bunny ran through a wall, he left a Bugs-shaped hole, rabbit ears and all. What does a Jesus-shaped hole look like? You got it: apostle, prophet, evangelist, shepherd, and teacher. Each of these leaders plays a vital role in equipping believers with a specialty so that they become a balance of the five roles. That's why Paul said these leaders are given "to equip the saints for the work of ministry, for building up the body of Christ, *until we all attain to ... the measure of the stature of the fullness of Christ*" (Eph. 4:12–13). Last time I checked, the whole church hasn't attained that fullness yet.

These roles have been given until we attain it. Therefore, I think we're gonna need these roles to stick around for a bit, until He comes back. If people see just the pastor-only model, they mistake Jesus's leg for the whole body. But when all five roles operate, the church's other three limbs will begin to be built up and attain Christ's stature in the world.

IF IT'S GOOD ENOUGH FOR VOLTRON, IT'S GOOD ENOUGH FOR ME

The church is a bit like *Voltron: Defender of the Universe*. Voltron featured a team of five young pilots who each controlled a giant lion vehicle that combined to form Voltron, a super robot as big as a skyscraper and nigh invulnerable. (Yeah, it's an eighties thing.)

On their own, each of these lion robots, cool as they were, got their metallic butts kicked by aliens. For some reason that only the modern church could relate to, the five pilots repeatedly tried taking on said aliens individually before finally uniting to form Super Robot Voltron. Now, I was only eight when I watched this, but every day I knew their modus operandi was doomed. So I just waited till they got their cans kicked enough till they decided it was time to press the red button, uniting them into (step back) Voltron, Defender of the Universe. Once Voltron took shape, alien mutants got cut down, massive energy swords flashed, some alien chick screamed, and the universe got saved. Thus endeth the lesson.

It's tough for an evangelist to strike out on his own when he doesn't know how to shepherd the community of people who get saved under his ministry. The pastor shepherds the people in the church while praying that he doesn't leak more out, but he struggles to get them to walk through the doors no matter how hard he tries. The pulpiteering teacher swashbuckles through the riggings of exegesis like Errol Flynn, but he has no clue how to care for his hearers when their lives fall apart. If we would take a lesson from an eighties Saturday-morning kids cartoon, we'd start to unite the five lions in order to create the image of Jesus, who would tower over our communities wielding the sword of the Spirit.

I believe that the biggest obstacle to this happening is the fact that we've had only one lion for so long. Tradition is at the wheel, and the Bible is in the backseat. When this issue is raised, pastors (who receive a paycheck from operating in a pastor-only model) look over at tradition in the driver's seat with a shut-up-and-drive expression. They need a ride, and the traditional model has been paying the bills. Besides that seminary invoice was a kicker! Alan Hirsch quoted Upton Sinclair as saying, "It is difficult to get a man to understand something when his salary depends upon his not understanding it."[3]

The real question is, is that what the *world out there* needs?

Maybe you've already been asking yourself that question. If you're not really a pastor, you're not sure why you haven't been able to just shut up and play along. You've wanted to be a good boy, with your hands folded in your lap, but you've been wired for something different. You were designed to fill the Doc Martens and kick a dent in hell, not hide behind a desk and pulpit. Let me repeat: you're not a shepherd. You're one of the other four roles. Like Ripley, as soon as you crawl into the exosuit cargo loader that you were made for, you'll start to kick some extraterrestrial butt again! Believe it or not.

KEEP REFORMING

By now you've probably started to label me as something, so I might as well grab a spray can and tag myself first. I'm solidly evangelical, and I bleed bibline blood. I got saved at a fundamentalist church in the eighties that was burning with the afterglow of the Jesus Movement. I devoured Bible teaching, bought a huge Puritan collection, and eventually pinned the "Reformed" name

tag on my shirt. I underwent metamorphoses of evangelical per-
suasions like a larva stuck in an endless looped cycle of pupa-grub
phase progression. Every time I thought I was ready to be a grub,
I reverted back to slimy larva. After a few years of thinking I
knew everything, I finally became aware of the vast universe of
theological truth that I was still ignorant of. Although I devoured
the Reformers, Puritans, Spurgeon, the mystics, the moderns, the
missionaries, I found I couldn't get enough. To this day, I still
derive more from Lloyd-Jones and Spurgeon than anyone else,
but I found that the more I learned, the bigger God got, rather
than shrinking so that I could get a good glimpse of Him. I got
an MA in Theology: Pastoral Studies, preached a lot, traveled
around, planted a church, and won the approval of many of my
colleagues.

But then I did something that you're not supposed to do. I
kept reforming. I kept reforming until it touched every area of my
theology, both theoretical and practical, including the chunk of
ice that I had been floating on.

But sometimes that's the choice we have to make: either be
"reformed" with what Lloyd-Jones called "smug contentment," or
make the choice to *keep reforming* until we are thoroughly biblical
in all of our theology. When that happens, labels stop fitting, a bit
like David in Saul's armor, because at some point, like Luther did,
you have to inevitably break free from some traditions.

The issue of justification by faith was pretty much nailed during the Reformation, but there are *other issues* in which the church
needs to *keep reforming*. The real question is whether most people
have the guts to make that commitment regardless of where it

leads. It might upset the establishment, but if you're not ready to do that, then you know nothing of the spirit of the Reformation.

The Reformation was just one of many reformations the church has needed throughout the centuries, and we're not done yet. Five hundred years ago, a brave group of monks and nuns flooded out of the monasteries, convinced that their reclusive cells were keeping the world from hearing the gospel. They lost everything, but the gospel spread like wildfire! Wesley and Whitefield defied the Church of England, threatened with defrocking as they shouted out the gospel of the new birth. The authorities didn't understand this "strange new doctrine" and believed that Whitefield and Wesley were obscene for preaching outside the church's four walls, but wherever those boys preached—be it field, cemetery, church, or chapel—unbelievers warned each other to stay away from the "soul traps."

I'm convinced that the same will happen again when we grab hold of the other four kitbags. I'm convinced that Acts will become a practical field manual and the Great Commission a realistic goal. Above all, I'm convinced that unless the church first changes itself, it will never change the world.

The term *reformation* referred to the church's need to reinvent itself *sola scriptura* until it was the same church in the book of Acts.

It was radical.

It was dangerous.

Praise God.

Does the church of today really resemble the book of Acts? If not, then it's time to get a'reforming.

IS THIS GONNA BE A STAND-UP FIGHT, SIR, OR ANOTHER BUGHUNT?[4]

Maybe you're thinking, *Yeah, but I don't want to change the way I do ministry. Maybe getting our metallic tails handed to us as solo lions isn't quite so bad as long as we can keep the machine running, make occasional repairs, and still show up to the fight.*

Let's face it, when we were kids we couldn't wait until the pilot in the black lion pushed the red button. You know why? We wanted to see some alien guts spilling. We wanted to see a win.

That's why we read books about the "good old days" in eighteenth-century England, or Lloyd-Jones's mini-revival in the dockside steelworkers' town in industrial South Wales, or even Southern California during the Jesus Movement when the Spirit moved through renegades.

Let me throw down the gauntlet. Like the Pharisees, we raise monuments to the prophets (Wesley, Whitefield, Roberts, Zinzendorf, Luther), but if they lived today, we'd recoil from them in horror. Go on … search your feelings … you know it to be true. Those "church history prophets" are your fathers, but you wouldn't join them in order to conquer the galaxy. Instead of being a Jedi like your fathers, you've been in the Empire locker room polishing your Stormtrooper helmet, hoping that the emperor notices what a good conformist you are so that you can speak at the next "Die Rebel Scum" conference.

The prophets challenged the status quo, broke out of the religious mold, and blazed a trail for the world to find Jesus. They burst apart the old wineskins as the Spirit fermented something potent within them that couldn't be contained. That's why we read books about them. When are we going to stop reading about or erecting literary monuments to them and finally jump headlong into the redemptive story unfolding in our time? We need more Gideons who are willing to smash the idols and desperately cry out, "Where are all his wonderful deeds that our fathers recounted to us?" (Judg. 6:13).

Have you been so busy keeping your job that you haven't been doing your job? Are you finally ready to put down the book, reform your approach to church leadership, and unite all five lions by pushing the red button?

Go on, push it. You know you want to.

4

ROUNDING UP THE
UNUSUAL SUSPECTS

*And he gave the apostles, the prophets, the evangelists, the
shepherds and teachers, to equip the saints for the work
of ministry, for building up the body of Christ.*
Paul, Ephesians 4:11–12

*This frightening hour calls aloud for men with the gift of prophetic
insight. Instead we have men who conduct surveys, polls and
panel discussions. We need men with the gift of knowledge. In
their place we have men with scholarship—nothing more. Thus
we may be preparing ourselves for the tragic hour when God
may set us aside as so-called evangelicals and raise up another
movement to keep New Testament Christianity alive.*
—A. W. Tozer, *Keys to the Deeper Life*

It's no wonder we're moving so slow.
Keith Green, "Jesus Commands Us to Go"

Must go faster.
Jeff Goldblum, *Jurassic Park*

Having looked at the A-Team maybe you realize that the apostolic team is a crack commando unit wanted for a crime that they didn't commit, and it's not a scriptural violation to start thinking about involving biblical special teams. However, if you're not completely convinced yet, this chapter is going to try to bang the nail into the red glitter coffin for you. We haven't even touched on prophets yet, and that's probably got you just as freaked as the term *apostle* did. Not to worry. You're in good hands.

The A-Team monologue says you can call on the A-Team "if you know where to find them." That's the big if. This chapter is about finding the A-Team, because chances are you've never seen them in operation.

Because apostles and prophets are the unusual suspects, their roles need a bit of clarification. Like B. A. Baracus and Murdock, the prophets and apostles have been underground due to the "shoot on sight" mentality, or you've simply been calling them by different names. This chapter is going to outline the roles of the apostle and the prophet, how they function in the church and on the frontier, and what they add to the mix.

I've identified three major components of each role. Why three? I don't know, but I've also alliterated them, and I never do that. Maybe somebody will invite me to speak at a conference, because I hear you have to alliterate everything.

APOSTLES

Voltron was so last chapter.

But it's important for you to know that four of the components were a green lion, a blue lion, a red lion, and yellow lion. There was no pink. You're thinking the Power Rangers, and that's way too juvenile for a chapter as serious as this one. Anyways, the black lion was the leader of the team, the one who pushed the red button, causing the tail-dented lions to form into the almighty form of Voltron. What the black lion was to Voltron, or Hannibal was to the A-Team, the apostle is to the church plant. He's the guy who has rallied the troops and led the charge. He's gotten you in over your head after you swore out loud, "I ain't getting on no plane, Hannibal!" But beware. He has ways to knock you out and bring you along anyway. He's the team leader, and he's got a one-track mind for kingdom expansion.

Being an apostle is a scary job, but somebody's gotta buck up and jump out of the airplane first. This guy is the one to do it. Because the apostle needs to be fearlessly forward thrusting, God has kitted him out with three essential qualities: guts, gestation, and grit.

GUTS

When you parachute drop into enemy territory, you want somebody sitting next to you that has guts. Apostles are the commandos grinning ear to ear before they somersault out of the hatch on the airplane. A church planter gets off on this stuff and possesses an uncanny bolus injection of faith; he's got enough to go around for everyone. He's got to, because his zeal needs to be infectious.

Ever wonder about the first guy to go over the top of the foxhole in WWI and brave the whizzing bullets of machine-gun fire? In this holy war, it's the church planter who's first to tackle the trench wall and charge no-man's-land. Paul had this frontline aspect in mind when he said, "God has appointed … *first* apostles" (1 Cor. 12:28). They are over the top about going over the top. You could say that apostles, like the Marines, are the bullet stoppers of God's army, leading the charge and *taking ground* for the kingdom so that the army can roll in behind them and *hold ground*.

But where does the apostle get his guts? Fear is a constant bedfellow, and as with any paratrooper who has jumped a million times, the apostle still feels the butterflies tickling his stomach before the next jump. The apostle can be a naturally hesitant person and still be a church planter. That won't bar him from his calling. His bravery doesn't come from his temperament but is a direct result of the supernatural bolus of the spiritual gift of faith (1 Cor. 12:9).

By faith, apostles can see a church coming into being when it hasn't been planted yet. They can envision stuff that nobody else sees. Not to overmystify it; they simply have a rock-hard faith regarding what God is calling them to. Faith is defined as "the conviction of things not seen" (Heb. 11:1). They say things like, "You guys are gonna see amazing things," and "I can't wait to talk to you in a year when you've seen [fill in the blank]." Their confidence inspires others to jump with them or after them.

Paul was able to inspire people to follow him across difficult terrain in the face of martyrdom to plant churches in pagan strongholds. He'd set up shop in Athens, telling his team with a wink that the Athenians were about to get another new God. At this point they must have scanned the city's millions of idols and felt Paul's forehead. It must have been the same look Walt Disney got on that day in the

1950s when he dug a hole in Anaheim and told his board members that he was building an underwater "submarine ride." They must've thought he'd gone a bit Goofy. All they could see was a hole.

This partial insanity or precognizant vision also helps the planter to sense God working behind the scenes when it looks like the fight is all over and to anticipate God's next move. Sometimes the fire of their faith seems almost inextinguishable. While everybody else is running around in circles like Bill Paxton in *Aliens*, screaming, "We're all gonna die! Game over, man! Game over!" the planter is just starting to feel challenged. Other people think the ship is sinking. The apostle thinks the ship is becoming a submarine.

When William Carey went to India, he labored for twelve years before witnessing his first convert, Krishna Pal. You might have thought Carey would be discouraged during those twelve years, but he was a bullet stopper. He had crazy faith. When Krishna Pal converted, Carey penned these words in his journal:

> He was only one, but a continent was coming behind him. The divine grace which changed one Indian's heart, could obviously change a hundred thousand.[1]

When Krishna Pal was eventually martyred, Carey didn't quit. He knew God wasn't finished breaking new ground in India. He kept at it, convinced that a sovereign God had called him as a kingdom commando. That's the kind of faith you gotta have to jump out of an airplane, plant a church, and not wee your dungarees. Luckily, big guts are in the apostle's kitbag.

GESTATION

Don't freak out. I'm not talking about planters craving Häagen Dazs with pickles and anchovies. I'm talking about the length of time an apostle spends in his targeted area, the gestation period that grows a church from a twinkle in the church planter's eye into a fully formed church that's just learning to stand on its own two feet. Eventually the church will grow up and have its own babies, but don't get me all misty eyed.

Church planting is the apostle's specialty. When Paul tagged himself as an apostle set apart from birth (Gal. 1:15), he was saying, "This is what I was born for." A pastor can plant a church, but church planting is what the apostle does for a living. For this reason, it's important to differentiate between the *sending* apostle (like James in Jerusalem—Acts 8:14), who has the people and resources to launch planters, and the *sent* apostle like Paul, whose hard-traveling gig rivals that of a rock star touring from city to city. They are "men on the move" rather than "men on the spot."[2] Once they've got a taste of planting, they become spiritual adrenaline junkies, and planting churches is as addictive to them as getting a string of tattoos is to posers. Once a poser's been branded, he's already thinking about the design of the next inked masterpiece to wow and amaze his friends.

I like to call Paul a serial church planter. Like a serial killer, the serial planter's going to strike again. Paul embarked on his first missionary voyage from Antioch and planted four churches in two years, covering 1200 miles.[3] Paul would have had only a few months to plant each church. Therefore, God hardwires the serial planter with a shelf life to accomplish his varied mission and keep him moving. Otherwise he'll go bad and start to stink like the brown bag lunches left in the coat closet in elementary school. You can't keep him for the long haul because he's built for the short term. As God's crack trooper, he's been given a huge objective but a short leash.

In this way he differs dramatically from a pastor. Just when things appear to be getting good for a pastor (like when the church doesn't seem like it will implode at any moment, or when the church can finally pay a minister), it's time for the apostle to kiss Miss Kitty and ride off into the sunset. An apostle finds the comfortable lifestyle of a shepherd to be yawn material. Think of Paul's travel, trials, and shipwrecks. He stayed in any given location for as little as two weeks (as with the Thessalonians) and up to nearly three years (as with the Ephesians). He was like a combat infantryman who couldn't function for too long in civilian affairs and started getting twitchy until he got back out into the field, the only place where his life made sense. Once he got his first taste of planting, he'd been ruined for life.

When the apostle waves his last good-bye to his newborn baby church, he may leave some of his team behind to care for them, or he may carry the whole team in his wake. But beware. He may also have recruited some additional cannon fodder during his stay with you. From the moment the apostle arrives, he is already beginning to sniff out the future church planters he's going to take with him on the next mission when he departs for good. The church may be a premie, or a post-due baby covered with cheesy vernix, but the church planter's gestation is something he feels in his soul, and when it's time to go, it's time to go.

Let him go.

I say that because it's not always easy. It's clear from Acts 20 that this was as tough for the apostle as it was for the Ephesian leaders as they wept on the docks when Paul left. Don't make it hard on him. It's hard enough already. Church planting can be a hard lifestyle, sometimes ripping your heart out, but like Paul, the apostle must "not account my life of any value nor as precious to myself, if only I may finish my course and the ministry that I received from the Lord Jesus, to testify to the gospel of the grace of God" (Acts 20:24). Being a social animal, Paul couldn't end a letter without writing lengthy greetings to the long list of faces that God called him to leave behind.

The apostle's divine directive has been to raise up leadership who can take the church forward, further than he could have. The apostle is prophet, evangelist, shepherd, and teacher until he raises up his replacements, but nobody can do all of those well for a sustained period. Eventually, people who specialize in teaching, shepherding, prophetic gifting, and evangelism are needed to follow in his wake. He's a foundation layer and the others will come and build on it (1 Cor. 3:10).

GRIT

Not only is the apostle going to eat mouthfuls of gravel, but he's going to have to dig deep into it. He's a foundation layer, and digging foundations isn't like the aboveground task of framing a house. It takes sweat, pneumatic drills, and ripped muscles. The church planter has got to dig a work that is deep enough to hold a stable foundation for others to build upon. This means that he's used to the hard work it takes to set up a church. Many of the would-be church planters that I've come across don't expect the hard work it's going to take or have the stamina to stick it out. They imagine that it will be as easy as Costner's *Field of Dreams*: "If you build it they will come." Just get the church-planter fauxhawk, talk like Driscoll, and thousands will flock to you. When discouragements come (and they will), these guys lean their shovels against the shed and complain about the rocky ground being too tough. I can picture Mattie Ross approaching the apostle Paul like he was Rooster Cogburn and saying, "They say you're a man with true grit." Because church planting's less *Field of Dreams* and more *True Grit*.

Sometimes when you're digging, you hit clay. That's the time to grip the shovel and bite down, because digging a hole is hard work. I can guarantee that most ministers today couldn't keep up with Paul for more than a couple of weeks. Ask John Mark. Paul wore young men out and ate up hirelings for breakfast. After dealing with filthy conditions and bug-infested beds and being stricken with malaria off the coast of southern Turkey, John Mark tapped out at the foot of the dagger-peaked Taurus Mountains. Nobody had prepped him for the Ironman ordeal that is church planting. Apparently, Timothy and Titus were made of harder stuff. On the issue of circumcision, Paul felt that Titus could handle the persecution from the Judaizers, so he got to keep his smurf cap. Yet Paul judged Timothy tough enough to endure some of Paul's less celebrated rabbinical skills with a knife. Circumcision was the price Timothy paid for infiltrating the synagogues in his church-planting reconnaissance mission, and Paul made sure he paid his dues.

My friend and veteran Continental church planter Stuart Ollyot once remarked that God uses bullheaded men to plant churches. Then, he looked at me and said, "I can see those necessary qualifications in you." Touché! The fact is, the church planter is so convinced of his calling from God that he feels too legit to quit. My partner in New Breed, M. C. legend Dai Hankey, who planted on a rough council estate in the Welsh valleys, had a dead body turn up on the lot near his house and butt pickles at the bus stop outside his door. He apologizes in advance to guys who guest preach in his pulpit because their car windows frequently get smashed. Hard ground like that would be enough to tempt anybody to hightail and run. Years on, Dai's tenaciously gripping the ground, painstakingly inching forward with a mouth full of gravel, and planting numerous churches in the area.

Digging also means infiltration. It's hard when you hit gravel and clay, but clay is what you hit when you've gone deep enough to make a difference. You can't just move the topsoil around if you're going to plant a church. You have to infiltrate the community and plant at the heart of that community. I remember working behind the bar at Starbucks, knowing that if God continued my call to being a barista that the combination of a minister and the marketplace was unstoppable. (The world needs God and good coffee.) When I planted Pillar, Starbucks was the heart of the marketplace in my community in the UK. In urban Long Beach, it's the parks and community centers. Because that's where the people converge, that's where the apostle is likely to be found. Like Paul, church planters tend to be people persons, guys who can laugh, rub shoulders, and mix with ordinary people while still bearing an extraordinary calling.

Geraint Fielder's book *Grace, Grit, and Gumption* chronicles the unlikely characters that pioneered the Forward Movement in

Wales, a church-planting movement at the turn of the twentieth century. The church planters, including prize fighters, coal miners, and former thugs, did everything from erecting circus tents, to challenging roughnecks to fistfights, to rescuing prostitutes from the sex trade, to preaching on the open streets. They were groundbreakers because they had their fingers on the pulse of their culture. Here's one example:

> One Saturday morning in May 1891, in the unchurched and sprawling industrial area of East Moors, Splott, Cardiff, two men could be seen putting up a large tent. The older man of forty-five, John Pugh, was unused to swinging a sledgehammer and he had lumbago for a month. The younger man, Seth Joshua who was in his early thirties, was adept at the job. Just as they finished, one of the rough characters of the area passed by. He was curious as to what was going on.
>
> "Hello, guvnor, what is this, a boxing show?"
>
> "There is going to be some fighting here," said Seth.
>
> "When are you going to start?"
>
> "Tomorrow morning at 11 am."
>
> "Tomorrow's Sunday."
>
> "Well, better the day, better the deed."
>
> "Who's on?"
>
> "He's a chap goes by the name Beelzebub."
>
> "Never heard of him. Who's he?"

"O he's a smart one I can tell you. Come tomorrow morning."

"I'll be there."

"And strange to say, he was there," said Seth. "When I had given out the first hymn, 'All Hail the Power of Jesus' Name' he knew he had been caught. Beelzebub went over the ropes all right, for the chap was converted that very morning."[4]

Those guys met a hard-bitten and godless culture where it was at, and penetrated. They didn't whine like metrosexuals that the work was too hard and crumple into the fetal position, muttering, "Where was my father, and why didn't he love me?" Instead, these guys fought tooth and nail to keep a hell-bound generation out of the flames. The result was the revival of 1904–1905.[5] In the words of the great Guy Fieri, "It's on like Donkey Kong! Swing the rope, jump the barrel, save the princess!"

PROPHETS

Okay, let's be honest. These are the guys that everybody is afraid of. When the saloon doors open and these guys stand in the doorway, everybody stops playing poker, and the cigars drop out of everybody's half-open mouths.

Why so serious? Probably because we've never really met a real one. If we had, we'd relax. These guys are usually extremely down to earth and humble—when they are the real deal.

And they encourage the heck out of you. According to Scripture, encouragement is the major function of the prophet. In Acts 15:32 we see Silas "encouraged and strengthened the brothers with many words." I can say from personal experience that in the early days of a church plant, a word in season from one of these guys can tip the scales away from discouragement. If the apostle is built to spread out, the prophet is wired to build up.

Apostles and prophets make legendary spiritual WWF tag-teams, and Paul frequently conjoined them (Eph. 3:5; 2:20; 1 Cor. 12:28). Luke also clamped these two offices together with handcuffs. In fact, Paul and Barnabas are listed among the prophets in Acts 13:1–3, indicating that this was their role for many years until they embarked for the mission frontiers and became apostles. It may have been advantageous to turn prophets into apostles (and I myself started as a teacher, then evangelist, then pastor, before I became an apostle), but to quote Forrest Gump, these roles go together like peas and carrots.

Jerusalem consistently sent prophets to strengthen new works on the front lines. In Acts 11, after the apostles heard of the Gentile converts in Antioch, they sent Barnabas to investigate the situation, carry on the work of evangelism to the Gentiles, and establish a proper church plant. Barnabas, in turn, fetched Saul from Tarsus to partner with him. Luke wrote, "Now in these days prophets came down from Jerusalem to Antioch. And one of them named Agabus stood up and foretold by the Spirit that there would be a great famine over all the world" (Acts 11:27–28).

Riddle me this, Batman: why would Jerusalem HQ immediately send prophets behind the apostles instead of a pastor? Because they thought that the office of prophet was essential to establishing a solid church plant. The prophet primarily encourages and strengthens by making others aware of God's presence. That is a foundational need. Even on Pentecost, Peter testified of the rise of prophets who would see visions and dream dreams in fulfillment of Joel's prophecy. Further, Antioch was left in the hands of prophets when Paul and Barnabas embarked on their first church-planting voyage (Acts 13:1–3).

But what about today?

BRICKS OF THEOLOGY

You're probably wincing right now, desperately wishing I wouldn't open this package of stinky cheese. True, there are wackos out there accosting people and telling others who they should marry, discrediting the biblical office. Listen, if you need God to tell somebody else that they should marry you, then you're either too ugly, stinky, or creepy to be married. The prophet as a matchmaker is a myth that I'd like to see busted forever.

Things can get messy when you speak about spiritual gifts, because man gets his grubby fingers all over everything. But if you've not been experiencing the gifts of the Spirit, your church already smacks of man. You need this next section more than you realize.

A. W. Tozer summarized the reason why this is such a crucial topic:

> For a generation certain evangelical teachers have
> told us that the gifts of the Spirit ceased at the death

of the apostles or at the completion of the New Testament. This, of course, is a doctrine without a syllable of biblical authority back of it. Its advocates must accept full responsibility for thus manipulating the Word of God.

The result of this erroneous teaching is that spiritually gifted persons are ominously few among us. When we so desperately need leaders with the gift of discernment, for instance, we do not have them and are compelled to fall back upon the techniques of the world. This frightening hour calls aloud for men with the gift of prophetic insight....

Certain brethren have magnified one gift out of 17 out of all proportion. Among these brethren there have been and are many godly souls, but the general moral results of this teaching have nevertheless not been good.

In practice it has resulted in much shameless exhibitionism, a tendency to depend upon experiences instead of upon Christ and often a lack of ability to distinguish the works of the flesh from the operations of the Spirit.

Those who deny that the gifts are for us today and those who insist upon making a hobby of one gift are both wrong, and we are all suffering the consequences of their errors.[6]

Can you see why they called him a twentieth-century prophet?

Ephesians 2:20 is a skull-kicking verse that demonstrates the foundational role of a prophet, saying the church is "built on the foundation of the apostles and prophets." Now some would interpret that to mean the New Testament apostles and the Old Testament prophets, but I'm convinced that the entire context is New Testament, and the prophets Paul spoke of are his contemporaries. That's because six verses later he said that the mystery of Christ (God's plan to save the Gentiles) was "not made known to the sons of men in other generations as it has *now* been revealed to his holy apostles and *prophets* by the Spirit" (Eph. 3:5). Did you catch that? Paul was speaking about prophets of the New Testament variety. Luke mentions nameless prophets (Acts 11:27), Agabus (Acts 11:28), Barnabas, Simeon (Acts 13:1), and Judas and Silas (Acts 15:32). Paul said, "God has appointed in the church first apostles, second prophets, third teachers" (1 Cor. 12:28). Has our paradigm for church interfered with our proper exegesis of this passage?

In the same passage, Paul established Jesus as the chief cornerstone. This implies that the prophets and apostles were laid after and alongside the chief cornerstone of Jesus's ministry. The method of building any foundation was to lay the cornerstone first, then lay the rest of the foundational blocks in alignment with it, to keep the foundation true. Again, the metaphor points to New Testament prophets.

It's true that the foundation could only be laid once. But the text nowhere says there weren't more prophets and apostles coming after them. In fact, in Ephesians 4 Paul argued that FIST Leadership (including apostles and prophets) is essential to the further building up of the church "until we attain ... the measure of the stature of the fullness of Christ" (v. 13). Therefore, in context, Paul viewed the roles of apostle and prophet as foundational blocks in establishing the church universally until the end of the ages. Besides, as I said earlier, Ephesians 4:10-14 indicates that these roles are needed to bring the body of Christ to complete maturity. Last time I checked, we weren't there yet.

Many people struggle with the idea of a New Testament prophet because the canon of Scripture is closed. Their concern is that a license to create biblical literature is being handed out with the title. We fail to remember that the Old Testament is packed with prophets who made cameos in Israel's history and never wrote a line of Scripture. They spoke into the moment. This string of pearls kicks off with Enoch (Jude v. 14–15) and is followed by Deborah (Judg. 4–5), Gad (1 Sam. 22:5; 2 Sam. 24:11–19; 1 Chron. 29:29; 2 Chron. 29:25), Nathan (2 Sam. 7, 12; 2 Chron. 9:29; 29:25), and others. There were unknown prophets in the days of Eli (1 Sam. 2:27–36) and Gideon (Judg. 6:7–10). Under Samuel there were schools of prophets (1 Sam. 10:10–12; 19:20–24); and Scripture also shows us the "man of God" from Judah (1 Kings 13), Ahijah (1 Kings 11:26–40; 14:1–18), Shemaiah (1 Kings 12:21–24; 2 Chron. 12:1–8), Iddo the seer (2 Chron. 12:15; 13:22), Azariah (2 Chron. 15), Hanani (2 Chron. 16:7–10), Jehu son of Hanani (2 Chron. 19:1–3), Micaiah (1 Kings 22), Oded (2 Chron. 28:8–15), Huldah the prophetess (2 Kings 22:12–20), Uriah (Jer. 26:20–23), Jahaziel (2 Chron. 20:14–17), Eliezer (2 Chron. 20:37), the prophetic school of Elisha (2 Kings 9:1–13), Zechariah son of Jehoiada (2 Chron. 24:20–22), the "Man of God" who forbade Amaziah's league with Israel (2 Chron. 25:7-10), the unknown prophet who rebuked Amaziah (2 Chron. 25:15–16), and another unknown prophet who encouraged and rebuked Ahab (1 Kings 20:13–15, 35–43). Similarly prophets that are walking around today may speak into the moment but don't write Scripture. That said, their messages better not violate Scripture but be tested.

Whew! Is your brain bowl cracked yet? Okay, you can take your hard hat off now, back to the non-noggin-bogglin' level of Sid and Marty Kroft–level theology.

All of that theological wrangling simply to rope this steer: the role of the New Testament (lowercase p) prophet is essential to foundation laying because of what the Holy Spirit has dropped into his kitbag: God-centeredness, gumption, and gift development.

GOD-CENTEREDNESS

To understand the role New Testament prophets play, you only have to think about Old Testament prophets. They pointed people to Jesus. The New Testament prophet is there to glorify Jesus, lifting the congregation to focus on Him once again. Because, like John the Baptist (greatest of the prophets), the prophets' primary job is to point to Jesus, they tend to be humble people who don't honk their own horns. Instead, they decrease themselves so that Christ may increase.

If you've ever seen the guys on the street corner with the giant foam fingers pointing you to cheaper insurance, then you'll understand that humility comes with the job. They are called to constantly point the big finger at Jesus and can't be bothered with worrying about what you think of them. Many people think they're freaks, and they've learned to live with it. They just put their iPod earbuds back in their ears and keep listening to God. Their overriding concern is that the congregation and leadership are laser focused and locked on Jesus. Sometimes they bring comfort, other times rebuke—but the purpose is always the same: to turn people back to God.

The prophet is a constant reminder of God's presence in the midst of the church. Paul said that when somebody prophesies, even the unbeliever will know that "God is really among you" (1 Cor. 14:25). Therefore, the prophet fulfills the dual function of bringing a sense of God's presence to both the lost and the found. They tend to be spiritually minded ministers who yawn through board meetings and cut through the red tape. Their constant underlying meta-message is, "Where is God in all of this?" They are constantly redirecting the other leaders back to God, factoring Him into church problems, re-gauging the thinking of everyone around them, or asking others to pause and hear His voice. After the Jerusalem council, when many difficult and controversial issues were created by the Judaizers, the believers simply needed to hear the heart of God again. Guess who they sent to Antioch? You guessed it: prophets (Acts 15:32).

GUMPTION

The prophet was, is, and always will be an unpopular role. In the Old Testament, the prophet exposed the lies that Israel hid behind to say everything was all right. Hirsch and Frost said that "a true biblical maverick acts in a prophetic manner by exposing the lies that the dominant group tells itself in order to sustain its shared illusions—and all groups, including the church, have them."[7] He's a straight shooter, and as such, he tells it like it is. He gives guidance that is often encouraging, sometimes at cross-purposes with personal agendas, but always uncannily wise. Sometimes he will say things that others have been thinking but haven't yet voiced, confirming God's guidance on an issue. Because the prophet brings God's heart on issues, people, problems, and ideas, he often changes the atmosphere of the room when he discharges his burden.

Therefore, insecure pastors don't dig having them around. The traditional model sees the pastor as the guy who has the monopoly on sharing the vision with others. In this sense, a prophet on your leadership team is a game changer. Nobody can claim that they have an exclusive batphone to the commissioner in heaven as they might in the pastor-only model. Instead, the prophet makes it easier to seek the face of God together as a team.

Having gumption, however, comes with an occupational hazard. Being gumption-filled opens you up to people thinking you're bologna-filled. Sometimes the prophet is the only one in the room who feels a particular way. For this reason, being a prophet can be lonely. In such cases, the prophet is aware that he's not infallible; he knows he can get his wires crossed, but most prophets who exercise their gift know they're knuckleheads like the rest of us, and have learned to treat Christ's bride with caution and to guard against letting personal opinions masquerade as "vision." Because the prophet walks a lonely road, he needs the encouragement and brotherhood of the team leadership. If he's a biblically legit prophet, and not somebody engaging in spiritual cosplay, he will be a team player.

I was blessed in my experience with prophets. My wingman in planting Pillar was an older guy named Jeff. Moses had Jethro. I had

Jeffro. Jeff was a veteran church planter in his sixties with nothing to prove, yet nothing to lose. His humility, wisdom, insight, and burden were a necessary component in what God did in the early days. I can remember the first night when I recognized his gift. He never showed up with a name tag that said, "Hi, my name is Jeff," with "prophet" written underneath. Instead, when he prayed for people, it kinda just happened. One night early in our underground team-building phase at Pillar, Jeff asked if he could pray for my wife while she was making coffee and tea for everybody in the kitchen. As she stood by the coffeemaker, he very tenderly laid hands on her and breathed out the most insightful heart-melting prayer about our undivulged infertility issue, expressing the Father heart of God toward my wife's brokenness. I stood there amazed as her tears began to fall. That night something changed in our situation and the way that we dealt with it. Funny thing is, I'd never heard my wife articulate her own heart so eloquently regarding our infertility. Weirder still, nobody in the room even knew our condition—we'd never told anyone. But God had.

It takes guts to be a prophet. When God gives you the big 'uns, you have to have the guts to take your tested burden to the leadership and appear to look the freak. Remember Agabus in Acts 11:28? He prophesied a famine. One day, just before our annual vision meeting, Jeff called me requesting to share a big prophecy. "I've never gotten a big one like this before," he said on the phone. He said the Lord had shared with him that an economic crisis (his exact words) of global proportions was going to hit soon. People were going to lose their jobs and be unable to pay their mortgages, and businesses would close, making it tougher for people who lost their jobs to get new ones. The places that people looked to for security were going to dry up. Jeff's burden was that the Lord was sharing this with us so that we'd be looking to Him for security instead of trusting in uncertain riches. That way, when the economic disaster hit, we wouldn't be panic-stricken like the rest of the world but would be consistently pointing people to the Lord with the unshaken confidence that this was no surprise to Him.

I paused on the other end of the phone. Because it sounded a bit weird, I tried to dissuade him. "Don't you want to share this in your small group?" Which was another way of saying, "Not sure I believe you … sounds freaky … the fewer people you tell, the less mess for me to clean up later." Jeff humbly and gently responded, "No, I think it's for everybody, but I'll do whatever you want with it." I knew Jeff would sit this one out if I asked him. After a quick Nehemiah bullet prayer, the Spirit prompted my heart to let go and give the green light. I knew Jeff, and he'd proven his integrity, although to anybody, including himself, this sounded a bit wonky.

As a result of not quenching the Spirit we got the blessing of seeing God at work, steering His people through adversity and preparing them as He did in Antioch for a coming famine. I can't tell you what something like that does for a young church plant. By the way, that was the first and only time while I was at Pillar Community Church that Jeff got a big 'un.

GIFT DEVELOPMENT

If the gifts bring a sense of the presence of God into your midst, then the prophet tends to stir up the gifts of others. It's just another way the prophet ensures that God is being factored into the mix. A lack of activity of the Holy Spirit in your midst will bug the prophet. It's not that he has an agenda to whoop up a Pentecostal Blues Brothers church frenzy, complete with guys double back-flipping on trampolines—it's just that he wants everybody to authentically experience God. He's not happy for God to be an abstract subject or for the worship of God to be coldly mouthed in boredom. He will encourage others to listen to God, find their gifts, share what God has put on their hearts, and step out boldly in faith.

Like Isaiah and Jeremiah, he will refuse to watch people pay lip service to God while they write Him out of their daily lives. Watching people playing games with God gets under his skin, and so he will serve as an irritant to those that are at ease in Zion. His message to all is to "seek the Lord today while He may be found." He's a bit like Morpheus in the Matrix. He wakes people up and points their gaze to penetrate through the Matrix. Like Moses, he enables an Aaron. Like Samuel, he guides and equips leaders like Saul and David.

WHAT THE HECK?

I know what you're thinking. You don't really want to open up this can of worms.

Fine. But you'll catch more fish when you do.

Remember that prophecy, according to Paul, is also an evangelistic gift so that the lost will know that God is among you. Paul's exhortation? "If [our gift is] prophecy, let us prophesy in proportion to our faith" (Rom. 12:6 NKJV).

Regardless of whether we've chosen to give them these titles, God has a way of raising people to do these very things whenever He's at work. I'm not so sure it even matters if we call them prophets, as long as the speaking of God's heart is done. But I'm convinced that it's going to make a whole heck of a lot more sense when we know what the Spirit of God is up to so that when He moves, it doesn't freak us out to the point of us quenching His activity.

I'm hoping the prophets and apostles out there will experience liberation as you discover the nature of your gifting. Perhaps you'll realize you were never a pastor or shepherd at all. You were one of these other two guys. There are five flavors to choose from when looking at serving the Lord full-time. What's your flavor?

In the pivotal "Neo starts kicking butt" scene in *The Matrix*, the following dialogue illustrates what happens when a Christian finally embraces the role God has called him to:

> Trinity: What's happening to him?
> Morpheus: He's beginning to believe.
> Trinity: Believe what?
> Morpheus: Who he really is.[8]

My hope is that God is waking up some prophets out there. If you're a Morpheus, it's time to rise up for Zion, because there are some Neos out there who need you.

THE THREE AMIGOS

As for you … do the work of an evangelist, fulfill your ministry.
Paul to Timothy, 2 Tim. 4:5

He securely led his fold, so that the wolf might never harry.
He was a shepherd and no mercenary.
Chaucer, *The Canterbury Tales*, lines 512–14.

This unity does not imply a drab mechanical sameness,
but a unity in variety, a unity in diversity.
Martyn Lloyd-Jones, *Christian Unity*

Maybe I am not meant for these duties. Cooking duty. Dead
guy duty. Maybe it's time for me to get a better duty.
Nacho Libre, *Nacho Libre*

"Wake up, Neo. The Matrix has you."

There is an old saying that the fish is the last one to notice the water. What if we are blind to the church structure system that we are swimming in because it's become so normal to us?

Did you know that the statement "What if I told you that none of this is real?" never occurs in the Matrix? It's a made-up paraphrase of something Morpheus said. Yet everyone thinks they remember it. Furthermore, what if I told you that the whole leadership structure of the Western church is more traditional than biblical? Not real. Made up—somebody's misprogrammed understanding that we've simply been replaying over and over without question. Why do we have so many different structures of leadership within Christianity, making it possible to swing from the Baptist trapeze to the Presbyterian rung? If we could let go of our white-knuckled grip on some of our traditional systems for a mere second, we'd begin a descent into the safety net of the biblical framework laid out for us in God's Word. Until we step outside of the paradigm that we're in, there is a danger that we'll fail to understand how it was all rigged up in the early church.

"You think that's air you're breathing?"

I want to introduce a virus into the system. Crash the mainframe and then reboot from the Bible up. Press F1 if you're ready, because a biblical reexamination is the only way to ensure that we're running in safe mode.

Once you understand the following other three roles that make up the apostolic team, your mouth will start watering for a return to New Testament leadership. When the disabled body of Christ regains its disused limbs, we'll start stretching out our hands and be made whole. Because, frankly, we're so lame that it's rip-off-the-ceiling-tiles-and-lower-ourselves-down-to-Jesus time. Only by looking at what the Head has set up can we begin to function again as the dynamic body of Christ.

If apostles and prophets are foundation layers, think of the following three amigos—the evangelist, pastor, and teacher—as the framers, roofers, and plumbers necessary to build up the body so that the apostle can be propelled to the next frontier. By the time Paul was living Acts 20:4, he was skilled in traveling with a mobile team of interchangeable house builders.

EVANGELISTS: ANTI-ZOMBIE SHOTGUN-WIELDING COWBOYS

In the sixties and seventies there was a flood of hippies coming to Jesus known as the Jesus Movement. At the epicenter of that cultural shakedown was Chuck Smith, founder of Calvary Chapel of Costa Mesa. But there was also another figure, an unsung hero of the Jesus Movement. His name was Lonnie Frisbee, and he was an evangelist. It was said that they came because of Lonnie and stayed because of Chuck. In a *LIFE* magazine story done at the height of the Jesus Movement, there is a photograph of Chuck and Lonnie standing in the water, both with a fist raised high in power, testifying to the power and grace of God. That snapshot embodied the powerful chemical combination of an evangelist-teacher team and the exponential dividends that come through ministry tag teams.

If Jesus fires the apostle as a mortar round to bust up the ground, then the prophet is a sniper who aims for the heart. That leaves the evangelist as the guy packing the shotgun. Why does every church need an evangelist riding shotgun? We've all seen churches that seem to have everything going for them—warm fellowship, stimulating teaching, competent pastoral care—but they don't impact anybody outside their four walls. That would never happen if they had an evangelist riding in their posse.

He rides with the team to keep an eye out on the horizon for some new cattle to lasso and brand out in the open range. The evangelist in your midst will constantly herd the huddling Christian cattle out of the corral and rustle them up to ride out into the wild frontier. In addition to carrying a six-shooter and some rustling rope, he comes equipped with the qualities of being constrained, convincing, and compassionate.

CONSTRAINED

Evangelists are constrained. Half of the time they'd rather not be out there. The most anointed street preacher prays with tremulous voice and shaking hands right before the gate of the bull pen swings wide. But then he roars like a lion. To all on the streets he appears fearless, but he has to screw up courage every time he steps out onto the high wire. If it wracks his nerves, then why does he do it? He can't help it. The love of Christ constrains him (2 Cor. 5:14).

Most people think of the evangelist as a frontline first-person shooter because he's constantly looking outward. The evangelist has a double-barreled approach, however, because he also builds up the body of Christ by equipping them to evangelize and by recruiting future soul winners. It's not by accident that he is mentioned third in the list. He's a linchpin between the church and outsiders with a responsibility in both directions. On the one hand, he faces outward, beckoning outsiders to come in; on the other hand, he faces inward, beckoning the insiders to go back out.

He equips the saints to do the work of the ministry (Eph. 4:12). Therefore, he's gonna bug you about giving up some of your free time to join him, because he's obligated to drag you along with him for training. You may run when you see him coming, but you can't hide. He knows that reaching the lost isn't your first priority. But God has made it his first priority. Like you, the evangelist doesn't always want to be out there either, but if he wasn't out there, you wouldn't be at all. Necessity is laid upon him, and his gut clenches when he stops so that he's miserable. With Jeremiah's pent-up fire raging in his bones, he cries with Paul, "Woe unto me if I don't preach the gospel." There is an old hymn that voices the mind-set of the evangelist:

> *We bear the torch that flaming*
> *Fell from the hands of those*
> *Who gave their lives proclaiming*
> *That Jesus died and rose.*
> *Ours is the same commission,*
> *The same glad message ours,*
> *Fired by the same ambition,*
> *To Thee we yield our powers.*
> *O Father Who sustained them,*
> *O Spirit Who inspired,*
> *Saviour, Whose love constrained them,*
> *To toil with zeal untired,*

From cowardice defend us,
From lethargy awake!
Forth on Thine errands send us
To labour for Thy sake.[1]

Jesus has hardwired him like Rocky Balboa to keep lifting him-self up off the mat and stagger straight back into the cement-filled gloves of Clubber Lang. And every time you watch him, you feel as pumped as you do at the end of a *Rocky* film, ready to climb into the ring.

A pastor friend of mine is a born evangelist. One night he was hanging out with about four other pastors who were telling jokes. Not wanting to waste this powerhouse of talent, he suggested that they head down to an entertainment zone and evangelize. They went, people got saved, and the four guys were gob-smacked. They went reluctantly with him at first because they didn't want to seem unspiritual, but they were glad that God put a gospel-wielding nut in their midst. They would never have witnessed souls saved that night without an evangelist.

Constrained people make the people around them feel con-strained too. For this reason, carnal Christians often resent the evangelist. They call him "over the top." They mutter, "We can't all be like him," or "It's just not what God has called me to do." But unless somebody challenges us to get out of our comfort zones, we'll see church as simply catering to our yuppie lifestyles rather than being a radical call to take up the cross of shame for the sake of others. As the church moves outward, people become more like Jesus than they were before.

Are you getting it yet? Each of the five roles pulls on the average believer to do something that he wouldn't normally be equipped or constrained to do. When you don't feel like getting out of the corner and taking another beating from skeptics, the evangelist is there to ding the bell again for the next round. When the church is insular, the evangelist spins the telescopic lens outward again. This is the effect Apollos had when he arrived in Corinth. Aquila and Priscilla held the role of teachers, and they'd been strengthening the believers after Paul had embarked for Ephesus, but when Apollos came on the scene, he got things stirred up again in Corinth and swung their eyes back out to the lost. The stagnant church was motivated, there was a second wave of evangelism, and as Paul put it, "I planted, Apollos watered, but God gave the growth" (1 Cor. 3:6).

CONVINCING

Evangelists don't have to be cool. I've seen the geekiest nerds on the planet win people to Christ. It's not about making Jesus look good (lucky Him—what would He do without us?). Paul wasn't very cool in Corinth. He wrote them reminiscing about how his speaking ability sucked: "And I, when I came to you, brothers, did not come proclaiming to you the testimony of God with lofty speech or wisdom" (1 Cor. 2:1). Perhaps he had a stutter like Porky Pig or a dialect like Foghorn Leghorn. But although he wasn't cool, there was a demonstration of the Spirit's power.

And that made all the difference.

The evangelist isn't called to knock 'em dead with his oratory, but there will be something about him, an air of authority that convinces and convicts. That's the Spirit! Billy Graham had it back in the day. So did Moody, Whitefield, Wesley, and Spurgeon. Spurgeon was often ridiculed for his country dialect and his blue polka-dotted cravat. Moody's crude American speech was mocked in highbrow Britain. Yet these men were anointed soul winners. Given a choice, I'd rather win souls than preach well. Mark it down, wherever a man wants to appear clever, the Holy Spirit backs off, but wherever a man's chief desire is to emulate John the Baptist by proclaiming the way, showing the way, and getting out of the way, shouting, "Look at Him!" the Spirit gives his voice a spiritual hi-fi boost.

Although Moody was a very intelligent man, he spoke simply so that people could understand him. He felt that gospel clarity was essential to salvation and impressing people wasn't. It's said that when Moody was invited to speak at Cambridge, the global seat of prestigious academic learning, he refused the temptation to appear respectable and began his sermon by saying, "Don't think that God don't love you, 'cause he do." The Spirit rushed in, and before the day had ended, he'd managed to reach the highbrow, blue-blooded young British academics. Tears, conversions, and prayers followed him on that tour, not to mention the triggering of the missionary revival resulting in the salvation of the Cambridge Seven (including C. T. Studd) that sparked a revival in the interest of world missions.

Why? Because people were being convinced by the Holy Spirit, not by Moody.

An old preacher once said, "You will never convince anyone else unless you've been first convinced yourself." If you're not convinced of the reality of hell and the passion of a crucified, risen Savior who gave Himself to rescue us from it, then you may be a fine orator, even a pulpiteering legend—but you won't save souls. In order to have fire in the pews there must be fire in the pulpit. Fire in the pulpit comes from a fire in the heart. A fire in the heart comes from the coals of the altar, and that can only be had alone with God.

Perhaps this is the biggest challenge to anybody who takes up the mantle of an evangelist. A preacher was once asked after a mighty delivery of the gospel how long it had taken him to prepare. His response was that to prepare his sermon had taken a few hours, but to prepare the *preacher* had taken his whole life. There is no shortcut to being convincing. Conviction is a hard-forged weapon, heated in the furnace of our hearts and beaten with the painful blows that fell on Jesus's back for the love of sinners.

COMPASSIONATE

When evangelists eyeball people, their hearts often break. They see people as Jesus saw them and regard nobody from a fleshly point of view (2 Cor. 5:16). It is said that Whitefield could never preach about hell without crying, and Keith Green wept as he sang, "Do you see, do you see, all the people sinking down? Don't you care, don't you care, are you gonna let them drown?"[2]

Paul described this compassion as Christ "pleading through us … be reconciled to God" (2 Cor. 5:20 NKJV). The evangelist's heart aches for the lost to return to God. Jesus sobbed, "O Jerusalem, Jerusalem! … how often would I have gathered your children together as a hen gathers her brood under her wings, and you were not willing!" (Matt. 23:37). That's what makes the evangelist grab a boomstick against the walking dead—he wants to put them out of their misery.

Wales is a rough place, and after being put in the hospital by
a rugby player on the streets less than six weeks after I arrived, I
learned a little respect for those who minister there. Pillar Church
had a tattooed recovering alcoholic for a street preacher. I went
and hit the streets with him for nine months straight, but one day
still stands out to me. A half-drunk heckler was ranting blasphe-
mous things about Jesus while he preached. As his mannerisms
got increasingly violent, I anticipated that my black-belt preacher
was going to have to fight for the right to continue. Instead, when
my eyes locked onto my evangelist, tears of compassion were running down his face. He was broken by the Holy Spirit's pain for
that man.

"Why should I listen to Jesus?" the heckler raged as he stormed
off, punching a street sign. The downtown street echoed with a
voice broken with emotion: "Because He loves you, mate." That
day, that city saw Jesus reaching out to a man lost in rage and
addiction. I wonder if that man walked home to his room and
broke down in repentance under the conviction of the Holy Spirit.

Most evangelists have a past where the wells of their compassion were dug deep. John Newton's depth of compassion for
down-and-outers was drawn up from his own years at the bottom
of the barrel. After he'd spent much of his earlier life raping, mur-
dering, and beating slaves, there was no dark corner people could
hide in where he hadn't already gone. Because the evangelist has
been forgiven much, he loves much.

If that's not the case with you, then you need the evangelist in
your midst to stir you up. Spend some time with one. Poke and
prod him. See what makes him tick. Put yourself in his way, and

volunteer your time to ride shotgun next time he's on mission. You'll never be the same.

The evangelist I worked with used to tell me, "Preach the gospel, mate, 'cause if you don't … I will!"

SHEPHERD: BA RAM EWE, TO YOUR CHURCH BE TRUE

Michael Palin plays eleven roles in one Monty Python film. Most pastors in the pastor-only model are attempting to fulfill their role and the other four roles as well. The Western church's setup is like a gig billing one headliner with no supporting acts. Somewhere along the line, we've equated the pastor with a CEO, administrator, visionary, and all-around power broker. Yet nowhere in the New Testament is the role spoken of in that way. For example, we read Paul's advice to Timothy as "how to be a good pastor" when it's actually one apostle writing to another. Paul's advice is given to troubleshoot an existing problem-infested church plant so that Timothy can get the heck outta Dodge and head back out on the road.

We don't really understand the role of a biblical shepherd.

The term *pastor* literally means "shepherd," yet it's funny how we attach so much esteem to being a shepherd in the West. When that term was used in the first century, it had the same stigma as a garbage man (ahem … sanitation engineer). People thought you were dirty and you smelled.

Everybody knows that shepherds lead the sheep to good grazing spots, check them for disease, clean them up, and protect them. This is a perfect metaphor for the shepherd who oversees the spiritual needs of the sheep. In other words, while the planter is out planting, the prophet is directing people back to God, and the evangelist is evangelizing, the shepherd is looking after the well-being of the sheep up close and personal-like. He can never take his eyes off them. He has to be watchful, warm, and warding.

WATCHFUL

As a missionary in Wales for twelve years, I gained a bit of familiarity with sheep. Sheep there outnumber human beings three to one. When I worked as a firefighter, the town I lived in was surrounded by green rolling hills stretching out into the distance, covered with white balls of cotton on four legs. Once when I was walking out in the wilds with my missus, we came upon a side-lying sheep, crazy eyed, breathing heavy, foaming at the mouth like Cujo. He was dying.

In the wilds of Britain it rains almost daily, and waterlogged wool is fatal to a sheep. Rainsoaked wool becomes so heavy that if the sheep falls over, it can't get back up. In a side-lying position, sheep can't expand their lungs properly, and they hyperventilate until they die. This usually takes a few hours.

When an old Welsh farmer came up the road, he knew what to do. We heaved all hundred-plus pounds of sheep onto his feet, and he frolicked away. The farmer shrugged. "That's why you can't leave 'em alone too long. It happens all the time."

Those of you in ministry know it to be true.

All I could think at the time was that I didn't want to reach into that mangy dreadlocked wool and pick that stinky thing up. Its wool was crammed with mud, urine, and feces. Here's some sheep trivia for ya. Did you know that a sheep doesn't wipe its butt? Maybe you've never thought about it. Feces gets so matted and ground into the wool on the back legs that the flies lay maggots into it. The maggots burrow into the feces-caked wool, and when they hit the sheep's living flesh, they don't stop. You know what sheep need?

You got it: a shepherd.

The shepherd has to cut that wool off and let fresh disease-free wool grow in its place. I can't think of many pastors who occupy the pulpit Sunday by Sunday who want to perform the spiritual equivalent in the pastoral care of their flock. Sheep are high maintenance and hands on. Before moving to Wales, I used to think that all you did was put sheep in a green field and leave them alone. Not so. To be a shepherd, you have to get down and dirty with the sheep.

I've met many teachers masquerading as pastors who are, as Spurgeon said, "at home among books, but quite at sea among men."[3] They complain about having to help their people in practical ways and consider preaching the best part of the job. These CEOs are attempting to reap the perks of the corporation without any of the HR responsibilities. By preaching to people weekly and leaving them to their own devices, they are essentially putting them out into the field, reasoning that if there is enough grass to eat, the sheep will be fine. That's how you tend cattle; God called us to look after sheep.

When John Wesley commissioned the circuit riders, they functioned as apostles preaching the gospel and establishing "societies." When Church of England clergy attacked him for sending nonordained yet gifted ministers, Wesley argued that nobody was shepherding the people in the established church. "Who watched over them in love? Who marked their growth in grace? Who advised and exhorted them from time to time? Who prayed with them and for them as they had need?"[4]

WARM

If you're gonna be cleaning a lot of sheep rear ends, then you'd better love people.

You're going to be called into situations that will turn your stomach, especially if you're reaching the unreachables. You're going to be dealing with addictions, rape, incest, domestic abuse, adultery, and the list goes on. To doctor the intimate hurts and histories of people's souls, you have to be relational.

Have you ever thought it strange that the three biggest characters in the Old Testament—Abraham, Moses, and David—were shepherds? God must have thought that cleaning the backsides of sheep was the best preparation for leading His people. That'd sure change seminary curriculums if we put it into practice. If I had been in Moses's place, I'd have laughed when God said He was gonna destroy Israel. Moses, however, had chased feces-ridden sheep across the desert for forty years, and he knew their tendency to get themselves into horrible predicaments by their own stupidity. So he begged God to be merciful. Abraham did the same for Sodom and Gomorrah.

John Pugh, a Welshman used heavily during the Welsh Revival of 1904–05, once remarked that the best pastoral training he'd ever had was working with the donkeys in the coal mines. He observed that if you can handle the stubbornness of a mule, then you can handle any awkward situation involving a Christian. To be a pastor, you have to be somewhat touchy-feely, caring for folk, weeping with them, and bearing with their failures. Jesus loves these people, and He will tell the shepherd to love Him through loving them: "If you love Me, tend My lambs" (John 21:15, author's paraphrase).

People need to know that the shepherd sympathizes with them, that like Jesus he is tempted in every way they are. Shepherds who segregate themselves from their sheep or elevate themselves above them quickly erode the trust of their followers. When trust breaks down, they hide their problems, and true transformation becomes near impossible. So remember that you, too, are stupid, and as an undershepherd you, too, need looking after periodically.

WARDING

Don't get me wrong. This guy isn't a cross between Captain Kangaroo, Mr. Rogers, and Ronald McDonald—even if he dresses like them. The shepherd has a cage fighter inside of him that claws its way out when wolves infiltrate the field. The shepherd will not abandon the sheep to predators.

A traditional legend about the aged apostle John illustrates this. In Ephesus, John had discipled a young man who became like a son to him. Upon his return from exile in Patmos, John inquired about his young pupil. The Ephesian elders broke the bad news that he'd joined a pack of bandits and was camped out in the caves that served as robbers' dens. John looked at the elders in bewilderment, asking, "And you let him go?" Before the night was out, the old man left and returned from the jaws of death with an arm around the wanderer.

As our Good Shepherd, Jesus flexes up and says He's willing to fight to the death for His sheep, and so will the true shepherd. When times get tough, a hireling runs away and looks for a bigger church, fatter paycheck, and a calmer pasture. Real shepherds look for a rock to put in their sling. They love the sheep like Jesus does, and they'll feed them, nurture them, and protect them.

Often the wolves come disguised as sheep, and the shepherd will watch their behavior over a period of time in order to discern whether they are friend or foe. In a church-planting context, the old saying is true: "Where there's light, there're bugs." The church is the brightest light there is, and it gets some of the freakiest people on the planet walking through its doors (outside of the Burning Man Festival). No more so than when word gets out that a non-established church is forming somewhere. People with freaky agendas creepy-crawl out of the woodpile and seek to steer the church. When we started Pillar, I got this reputation in my church for being a bit of a hatchet man. I was very strict about forbidding Christians from transferring over to us for the first two years. It was for protection. In a church-planting situation, a shepherd should maintain the core team and look out for their needs as they are ministering to others.

One final note about the shepherd: he has a weakness that sometimes gets in the way of his functioning as a warder, particularly when the threat comes from within. Because he deals primarily with caring for people's spiritual needs, he can easily fall into the danger of people pleasing. Even though the apostle Peter had been graced with the vision of barbecued pork, he fell into the trap of hypocrisy and people pleasing when the Judaizers came knocking in Antioch. Paul asked, "Am I now seeking the approval of man, or of God? Or am I trying to please man? If I were still trying to please man, I would not be a servant of Christ" (Gal. 1:10). Paul rebuked Peter to his face, as he recounted in Galatians. Having the balance of roles on a team will keep each role safe from its inherent weaknesses.

TEACHERS: SIT DOWN, WALDO, I'M HOT FOR TEACHERS!

On any given Sunday, most of the guys we call pastors mount the pulpit steps in their stylish blue jeans and designer collar shirts when the bright lights signal that it's showtime ... and they think they've shepherded. Not so.

They're not even pastors. They're teachers. The term *shepherd* is synonymous with *pastor*, and these guys don't do any shepherding at all. Many of the radio preachers and pulpiteers of large churches are really occupying the biblical office of teacher.

Think about it. Do they ever do the down-and-dirty work of tending the sheep, or are they hands off and impossible for the sheep to reach by telephone? On rare occasions their people may get to touch the hem of a garment and treat the occasion like a meeting with the Great and Powerful Oz. "Pastors" who occupy the pulpit Sunday by Sunday usually have little time left over for the flock, but the system demands we call them pastors. You know why? Because we have a one-man system, and that system says the guy in the pulpit is the boss.

You ready for more formulas? Here's some cheap college logic:

A. Preacher = Pastor

B. Pastor = Boss

Ergo

C. Preacher = Boss

We've backed ourselves into a practical corner by calling the guy who does the bulk of teaching the pastor. When Jesus told Peter to feed his sheep, He also said, "Tend My lambs." Because we imagine Peter to be a pastor "like us," we imagine that preaching is the main job of a shepherd. But the Scripture doesn't say that. Peter wasn't a shepherd or a pastor. He was an apostle. That's why Peter had evangelist, pastor, and teacher all rolled up into his makeup. Yet he was an apostle with the gift of teaching, and as you'll see next chapter, they had to shoulder all the roles for a limited time, so he was told to do the job of both a shepherd and a teacher. Nonetheless, we've made a whole system based upon our misunderstanding of these verses, and we've married these two roles into the pastor/CEO/boss.

Here's how you can tell whether you're a pastor or a teacher. If most of your time is taken up getting involved in the real-life problems and situations of the flock, then you're a shepherd/pastor. However, if most of your ministry is spent studying for messages and delivering Bible studies, you're a teacher and not a shepherd in the biblical sense.

"But I shepherd them by preaching to them," the objectors say. True. You teach them. You are a teacher. Any other questions?

In the Western church, if we acknowledge the role of teacher at all, we normally bust them down to the rank of private, placing them in a home study or adult Sunday school class, but we never imagine that the pulpit should be occupied by the role of teacher. That's because we've modeled the office of teacher to fit our existing church structure, rather than taking our cues from the biblical model. But if we adopt a team leadership with all five roles Jesus gave to the church, there is no reason *pastor* should equate to *boss*. There's also no biblical reason that the guy occupying the pulpit every Sunday should be boss instead of teacher. Paul said, "Having gifts that differ … let us use them: … if service, in our serving; the one who teaches, in his teaching" (Rom. 12:6–7). Paul continued his list by noting that those who are gifted in leading should do so "with zeal" (v. 8). The shepherd should take the lead in taking people by the hand, through counseling and discipleship, but the teacher takes the lead in the pulpit, bearing the lion's share of the preaching. Each leads in a different way.

How many pulpits are filled with guys who are able to teach but don't excel at it? I've heard many people say that their pastor (rightly termed) who stinks up the pulpit (wrongly placed) is "such a nice guy." He usually is, until the unthinkable happens. Up from the ranks comes a teacher whom the Holy Spirit has gifted to teach, and the King of the Mountain struggle ensues with all the antics of a first-grade playground. Everybody in that church knows that these guys should split the ministry between the pulpit and the touchy-feely counseling stuff. But in the Western church there is only one ring of power, and everybody wants the "Precious." Team leadership is fraught with problems only if you are jockeying for position, which the disciples did repeatedly until Jesus gave them enough whacks on the head with a spiritual two-by-four.

If your model isn't working, maybe you don't have the right model. Maybe we should submit to the FIST Leadership model laid out for us in the Bible. As every church-planting missionary eventually learns, culture must bow to the Scripture. Isn't it time that ours did?

A MALNOURISHED BODY

If all five roles are essential to the building up of the body, then the pastor-only model is tantamount to eating only one of the four food groups. The West's failure to ingest a proper diet has left the body malnourished, and the result is that we're unhealthy.

You may not be getting the pastor-only model. It could be the teacher-only model if the boss man at your church is a teacher. If you sit under a famed evangelist, then it's the evangelist-only model.

But do you know what happens when you let teachers run the church alone? You get a classroom. And when the church becomes a classroom, you start calling it a campus. Classrooms are really just places to hold audiences where people sit and listen. Listening is necessary, but is that all there is? Similarly, if a prophet runs the church alone, you get a circus. The balance of these five roles keeps the church…well…balanced.

We need to be instructed from the Word of God. Therefore God gave the church teachers. However, we also need to be doers. Therefore, God gave us evangelists to ride us out the gates. When we get back into the corral, we need to encourage each other by exercising our gifts among ourselves. Therefore God gave us prophets to stir up our gifts. Life chews people up, so we need shepherds to biblically counsel people, gently tending Christ's lambs. Lastly, there is a vast untamed pagan wilderness expanse out there. Therefore we need to look outward to the unexplored wilderness of missionary endeavors where Christ has not been named (Rom. 15:20–21). We need apostles to remind us that there are still unconquered frontiers and that we must go there.

Have you ever wondered why there are plural "elders" in the New Testament church? In the West the elders are either toadies to the CEO pastor who hope for preaching scraps to fall from the table, or they are there to make sure that the pastor doesn't get a big head, steal money, or sleep with your wife. What if the elders of the church were the apostle, prophet, evangelist, shepherd, and teacher? What if the multiplicity of elders in the first-century churches existed because these five roles were essential to modeling the full ministry of Jesus? Together they would keep the church in a correct nutritional balance. Each leader with a unique emphasis would create a healthy tension in the leadership team between five separate areas.

An eldership team needs to have each of these roles represented on it. Of course, an apostle may be shared by a large number of churches, as was the case with Paul. Therefore a church doesn't need to have one of these guys "in residence" at all times, but like Paul he'll keep checking in and checking up.

If a church lacks input from any of these leadership roles, it will become malnourished in that area. Ideally, all of the elders will have opportunity to teach, and Paul is clear that biblical elders should be *able* to teach, but the term *able* does not mean it's their specialty. The teacher gets top billing and does the lion's share of the preaching, but the others are supporting acts. Paul said if a man's gift is teaching, let him teach (Rom. 12:7). He didn't say, if a man's gift is teaching, place him at the apex of the pyramid. In fact, any of these five roles may be the "first among equals" who lead the ministry team. It doesn't matter, and the Spirit sets it up differently in various churches. In the days of Pentecost, Peter appeared to take the lead, and when he traveled away, James became the first among equals on the Jerusalem team. Likewise Paul led his missionary teams.

While I was doing my MA in pastoral studies, a seminary student asked, "How many elders should a church have?" The answer given was, "It depends upon the size of your congregation." But there was nowhere in Scripture that told me how many leaders I should have per congregant: one per ten? One per one hundred? One per thousand? What was the rule? I was confused. Today I'm probably still confused, but my answer would be much simpler. I would be working toward a minimum of five, for obvious reasons.

Don't get me talking about Voltron again.

6

SHOW ME YOUR KUNG FU

I planted, Apollos watered, but God gave the growth.

Paul, 1 Corinthians 3:6

Many of us are more capable than some of us …
but none of us is as capable as all of us!

Tom Wilson

Finding good players is easy. Getting them
to play as a team is another story.

Casey Stengel

Did you ever hear of the Seattle Seven? That
was me … and six other guys.

The Dude, *The Big Lebowski*

I KNOW KUNG FU

"Everybody was kung fu fighting! … It was an ancient Chinese art, and everybody knew their part."[1] Every kid growing up in the seventies feared the boy who knew karate. The answer to every chest-bumping conflict was, "Okay, show me your kung fu." Once, when my friend and I were walking down a back alley in our neighborhood, another kid leapt out at us and threw down an exaggerated Bruce Lee pose. With eyes bugging out and body so contorted that it reduced his size in half, he challenged, "I know kung fu! You think I don't?"

My buddy said no and opened up a can-o-whuppin' on him until he cried. Lesson learned: talking karate isn't the same as chopping karate. (Never mind that white kids in the seventies didn't know the difference between karate and kung fu.)

So far we've talked up some kung fu, but you need to see how the apostolic network works before you know how your team is meant to function. After spending the last few chapters showing you "Wax on. Wax off," "Sand the floor," and "Paint the fence," it's time to honor Mr. Miyagi and show you some karate. The best way to do that is to watch the apostles as they roundhouse through the book of Acts, while also observing Paul as he makes flying-kick comments throughout his epistles. Wanna see them bring it?

WHERE'S WALDO?

In *The Karate Kid*, Miyagi takes Daniel-san to the Cobra Kai dojo. That scene brilliantly illustrates that the philosophy and training of the Cobra Kai are in direct opposition to what Miyagi has been teaching. After challenging the entire dojo in the competition at Daniel-san's expense, Miyagi tells him, "Miyagi just save you beating for one month." Our lack of understanding of the Ephesians 4 model has affected our outcomes personally, structurally, and denominationally so that we've been getting karate kicked all over the chain-link fence.

Sometimes you learn the most from the fight that you got your butt kicked in. Let's just look at the areas where the enemy's Cobra Kai have introduced the foot of instruction to the crotch of understanding: personally, structurally, and denominationally.

PERSONALLY

Leaders will become frustrated if they don't do what they were designed for. Where are all the apostles, prophets, and evangelists? If the apostles didn't end up as frustrated misfit "pastors," they probably came on staff at some parachurch missions organization as pencil pushers for Jesus. If that didn't satiate their wild thirst for the frontier, they lit off for the mission field, or they stayed stateside, planting churches anyway. The prophets made their way to the charismatic and Pentecostal circles, where the gifts were welcomed. The evangelists gravitated toward the fundamentalist or evangelical circles they were saved in. The shepherds became professional Christian counselors that people would pay through the nose to see because the local leadership didn't value their training and insight. The pastor-only model had no place for them, whereas Focus on the Family did.

But just because teachers are running the show doesn't mean that the teachers in the pews are happy either. Imagine that a teaching-based church boasts a membership of twenty thousand people. Let's conservatively speculate that God gifted one per every hundred people as teachers. Do you know how many frustrated teachers you'd have in your congregation? You'd have two hundred frustrated teachers in captivity slowly atrophying because they're not doing what they were designed for. Like a killer whale in captivity, their dorsal fin has folded over, demonstrating the brokenness of a wild beast never meant to be tamed for circus tricks in a swimming pool. The result is that disused teachers with postgrad degrees take faculty positions at seminaries like pachyderms that migrate to elephant graveyards.

STRUCTURALLY

The Ephesians 4 leadership team is made up of radicals and conservatives. Every elder board needs a balance of those, whether it's in the church or the corporate world, but in Christianity we've pushed out the roles that make up the radical wing: the apostle, prophet, and evangelist.

So let me get this straight. The radicals aren't considered valid, while the two conservative roles (shepherd and teacher) are recognized? Wouldn't that explain a lot within the church right now?

In His wisdom, God knew that the church needed both conservatives and radicals. In fact the ratio is 3:2 in favor of the radicals. What should that tell you? Christianity is a radical movement. The conservatives are there to keep things safe.

Remember the migration of the prophets to the charismatic movement? The teachers to the seminaries? The counselors to parachurch marriage and family ministries and private practices? What would the church have looked like if they'd all stayed together?

Can you see the powerhouse of ministry that we'd be? Can you see the balance we'd have? Each of these guys left because they felt their way was the right way, instead of realizing that all five emphases were vital to the church's development. Here's the kicker; we'd look like the early church.

The teachers would have kept the prophets from the excesses of some of the Bozo movements among the charismatics, and kept them from becoming charismaniacs. The prophets would have added depth to the teachers and prevented them from boring the daylights out of people. The shepherds would have discipled mature disciple-making disciples who joined the apostles' brave rush over the top into no-man's-land, and the church would have been spared from wandering all these years in the wilderness.

The church regaining the biblical structure of Ephesians 4 would give it a T2100 endoskeleton causing it to function like a terminator programmed to "never stop, and never give up" until it fulfills the Great Commission.

DENOMINATIONALLY

Denominations are another way the church has gotten a butt kicking. Over the past centuries, as the five roles were scattered and the body of Christ fragmented, each of the five roles held a different part of the elephant. The Presbyterians grasped the part about the plurality of elders but fell short of understanding the true reason for the plurality. The Anglicans mimicked Paul's overseeing relationships with the churches he planted, but rather than forming an apostolic network, they formed bishoprics as elite super-pastors. The independents further fragmented because of their distrust of authority and settled into the pastor-only model.

God is forming a new breed of church from the various camps of unbalanced movements. The new breed of church has:

- the outward focus and forward movement of the global mission field and the domestic church-planting movement (emphasizing the apostolic).
- the manifestation of balanced and biblical uses of spiritual gifts from the best of the charismatic movement (emphasizing the prophetic).
- the evangelistic thrust of the fundamentalist and evangelical movements with the cultural sensitivity of the emerging movement (emphasizing the evangelistic).
- the training, expertise, and hands-on involvement of the Christian counseling movement, and focus on discipleship and personal spiritual growth (emphasizing shepherding).
- the doctrinal stability and clear gospel presentation of the Evangelical and Reformed movements (emphasizing teaching).

How do I know this? Because this is what I'm planting.

And I'm not alone.

LOVE YA, BABE—LET'S DO LUNCH

We've got some retraining to do in the dojo.

First lesson: whereas the Western church today is obsessed with *size*, the first-century church was obsessed with *reach*, and that made all the difference.

Miyagi's lesson about waxing cars and cleaning floors is intended to teach Daniel-san to get his center of balance from his core. "Karate here," he said, pointing to his heart. This is the heart of the apostolic kung fu.

You ready to learn the secret of "wax on, wax off"?

The first time out on a mission to change the world, Paul and Barnabas took John Mark with them, but that didn't work out so good. By Paul's third missionary journey, he was traveling with up to eight other guys (Acts 20:4), and the next time we glimpse Paul, he'd changed up again. Paul was like Mom's taxi, constantly picking guys up to drop them off later in another town. As he carried them across Asia Minor, they learned on the job. They picked Timothy up in Acts 16:3 after a painful operation to his nether regions, and then "as they went on their way through the cities, they delivered to them for observance the decisions that had been reached by the apostles and elders who were in Jerusalem" (v. 4). Networking wasn't just an eighties thing where your people called my people and did lunch. It was also first century.

Paul's network was Asia Minor, of which he states, "so that from Jerusalem and all the way around to Illyricum I have fulfilled the ministry of the gospel of Christ" and "but now, since I no longer have any room for work in these regions" (Rom. 15:19, 23). Before his arrival in Rome, Paul considered his network covered when he had planted churches in every major metropolis in Asia Minor and trained up a large network of apostles to continue the work. By the time he lost his head on the Appian Way, he'd set in place a posse of at least thirty-two pioneering missionaries who were ready to take his place as "sent-out ones." They had been trained to pick up where Paul had left off, and they were already doing it. These thirty-two names include Agabus, Apollos, Aristarchus, Artemas, Barnabas, Clement, Crescens, Demas, Epaphras, Epaphroditus, Erastus, Gaius, Jesus (Justus), John Mark, Lucius, Luke, Onesimus, Onesiphorus, Priscilla and Aquila, Secundus, Silas, Sopater, Sosipater,[2] Sosthenes, Stephanas, Timothy, Titus, Trophimus, Tychicus, and Zenas. That's why before he left Ephesus before getting locked up for good, he rented the school of Tyrannus for two years ... to train his apostles (Acts 19:9-10).

Paul knew he couldn't change the world by himself. He knew it was a team effort. At some stage he must have realized he was a Swiss Army knife.

THE SWISS ARMY KNIFE

Dai Hankey, the other punk of the two-punks-and-a-logo New Breed team, likens church planters to Swiss Army knives. Like a Swiss Army knife, apostles tend to have all the gifts necessary to run a church, but perhaps in one area they are particularly strong, such as in preaching or leadership. The apostle Paul was a prophet, evangelist, pastor, and teacher. As multi-tools go, the knife blade in the Swiss Army knife isn't half bad. The scissors and corkscrew, however, aren't the best by far. For one thing you need midget fingers to use the scissors, and you probably wouldn't want to do your Christmas wrapping with it unless you like cussing. In New Breed, we say that a guy's most obvious gift is his "big blade." Perhaps another area, such as administration or prophecy, is his magnifying glass—the tool gets the job done, but it definitely won't be fire scorching any ants when held up to the sun. He's usually performing duties that aren't quite his specialty in the beginning, but eventually when somebody comes along who can perform the role that he's not so good at, he breathes a sigh of relief that at least the scissor tool can go away for the time being.

Again, there is no predictable formula for what gifts the Lord will give in strength from one church planter to the next. For example, Timothy is exhorted to do the work of an evangelist (2 Tim. 4:5), although it wasn't his "big blade." It was the work he had to be reminded to work at. For Paul, however, evangelism was his long knife blade, his specialty. Eventually, we see him taking the lead in evangelism in the Paul/Barnabas tag team.

One of the reasons for constantly adding people to the apostolic team is because of their various gifts in different proportions. Church planters are like Jedi warriors. They can Force pull, Force leap, mind control, shoot glowing blue balls of lightning, and wield light sabers, but Jedi Knights each have a Force power they've learned to master. For example, Obi-Wan's special Force power is wisdom.

I've worked with guys who possess that spiritual gift in a proportion that far exceeds their other gifts. Anakin could absorb more Force power than any other Jedi, making him a pretty bad little Jedi boy. Qui-Gon could become a blue smurf spirit after being chopped in half and have conversations with Yoda. Yoda could see the future, another could heal, another could fight better.

Like Jedi with their differing force powers, one apostle might have a more prophetic gift, another a more evangelistic gift. Titus appeared more front line in the assignments that Paul gave him, while Timothy appeared to be less of an evangelist and more pastoral, straightening out problems where he found them. Peter appeared to be an uncanny combination of both. My preeminent gift is teaching. If I were planting with James, the apostle and pastor of Jerusalem, I would let him take the pastoral lead because shepherding was his prominent gift. Apollos would probably take the evangelistic lead on my team, and I'd follow his lead on those issues. Priscilla and Aquila, having been discipled by Paul himself, would undoubtedly be the greater teachers, so I'd shove a bun over to the side so that he could teach the men and she the women.

Because God has distributed differing gifts and temperaments, a complementary team is essential. When one member of my team was about to launch a church plant out of Pillar Community Church, he had an uncanny gift of leadership and was a solid teacher. There was one concern we both had: he was a shy guy. I asked Steve Timmis over a cup of coffee what he thought about it. Timmis responded, "He sounds like me. I'm an introvert. I wouldn't be too concerned as long as his team members can make up for his lack. Make sure he has a few extroverts on his team." The sooner you learn this valuable lesson, the better. Your team members make up for the giftings you don't have.

God sends you the backup you need based upon what you're personally deficient in. For example, if the scissors in your Swiss Army Knife suck, God will send you a scissor. If your corkscrew is too short to pop a cork, then God sends a corkscrew. What gift are you, the apostle, lacking? My main weakness was on the prophetic side, so God sent me a co-pastor who had that in huge doses. I stood amazed as I watched him in action, stretching the body in ways that I never could have. He was not the pulpiteer that I was, yet his sermons called to a different part of the believers. His preaching was tinged with a prophetic edge, and his messages focused more on a burden than exposition, and often caught things that I would have missed because he was thinking like a prophet rather than a teacher.

Think *The Fellowship of the Ring*. Think *Justice League*. Think any successful sports team. Each of them is chosen to work together because their individual strengths make up for another team member's weaknesses.

In Acts, when the Holy Spirit began moving in Antioch and the pagans started to believe in the gospel, the Twelve shipped Barnabas there. Arriving in Antioch, Barnabas encouraged the Christians and evangelized the lost. The result was "a great many people were added to the Lord" (Acts 11:24). Then, after he fetched Paul to Antioch, they both spent a whole year teaching the multitudes. Finally, there was the need for some specialist tools to come in, so we're told that "prophets came down from Jerusalem to Antioch" (Acts 11:27). Two years later, after the damage done by the circumcision group, the Twelve sent up two prophets, Judas and Silas, to encourage and strengthen the church (Acts 15:22–23). If we traced the order of the pattern of what roles God sent to Antioch, it would functionally look like this: evangelist, teacher, and prophet.

That pattern changes depending on the needs of the particular church. For example, it changed in Corinth (Acts 18:24–19:1), so we know it was in response to the needs of that particular situation instead of some rigid formula. After Paul stayed in Corinth for a year and half, he handed the reins over to Priscilla and Aquila, who possessed the gift of teaching. They then followed Paul to Ephesus and taught the new converts there. When Apollos showed up, Aquila and Priscilla ripped him a new theology and sent this ripping evangelist back to their previous post in Corinth. There he evangelized the Corinthians, and there was massive fruit as the church infiltrated the community again. In this case, the evangelist tool was needed.

Although Paul's major gift was evangelism, he couldn't be in two places at one time. Corinth needed evangelism … again; Antioch needed both evangelism and teaching; and then two years later, it needed prophecy. They were different church plants, and the sovereign God sent them backup to suit their need.

HOW THE NETWORK WORKS

Like "The Dude" says, this is the rug that really ties the room together.

Our network isn't simply a club that you join so that you can come to conferences and put our logo on your website and say that you belong to the New Breed posse. It has to be more practical. If you join our posse, you have to ride with us. Belonging to an apostolic network means that when you're planting a church, the other New Breeders in your network turn up and help you with the gifts you're lacking in.[3] If your worship leader sucks, I send you a guy who trains your worship leader for a month or two. In Pillar, my worship leader trained up three separate teams because we were planning future church plants. Rather than gunning for the next "big thing" of worship so that we could cut a CD and televise a "worship experience" complete with pyrotechnic explosions and acrobatic dwarves in VeggieTales costumes, our mind-set was more kingdom driven than empire building. Kingdom ethics come into this big-time: if I have two cloaks when my brother has none, it's a no-brainer. In this way, churches start to work together for kingdom expansion rather than empire building. Until that happens, you're just not walking in the footsteps of Paul.

We all know that worship leaders can be prima donnas who get worked up over somebody else getting to play every Sunday. With a sour spirit, envy and selfish ambition curdle hearts like rotten milk. But when a church practices the networking model Paul used in Asia Minor, it keeps your church carton from stinking. People who want to be used, get used. We use the prima donnas to lead worship in our next frontline church-planting venture. They're happy, and the planter is happy. He needed their gifts, and they weren't being used back at the ranch.

You need help setting up a corporation? We've got lawyers within the network who'll help you. You suck at math but need to balance the church's books? We've got a treasurer at one of our plants who'll train your math guy. And you need a math guy. Even Jesus recruited an accountant (Matthew), and He had less money than you. So you find the number-crunching nerd in your congregation who loves Sudoku and thinks math is fun, so that you can focus on your gifting (preaching, pastoring, evangelizing, or prophecy). People with that specific administrative gift within the network can help your geek squad, freeing you up to perform the duties of your ministry and, in the process, giving you your life back. Work smarter, not harder.

This also applies to evangelism. New Breed started when we planted out of Martyn Lloyd-Jones's church, Sandfields. The planter at the time was just finding his preaching legs and wanted somebody with a clear evangelistic gifting while he was still developing. I came once a month, and every time I preached, somebody got saved. That's when I began to notice that Paul was doing the same thing in the New Testament when he moved people around.

Dai was a drum and bass DJ/MC at a popular nightclub in the capital city prior to being a church planter. Dai loaded his kit up and did some outreach in a pub out our way. After the gig, we argued about paying each other. "Look, mate, this is New Breed. There's no money involved." That ended the discussion and set a precedent. New Breed is a hybrid of Don Corleone and the apostle Peter. Like Peter, we say, "Silver and gold I don't have, but what I have I give you." However, when I need a favor later, I may call on you mafia style. Maybe you've got a graphic designer, and I need a logo. It's all about bringing in your special team of crack troops who help you heavily hit an area.

Imagine Paul rolling in with his posse, a hand-picked, well-trained arsenal of ministry, ready to unload all of their firepower on your target zone. When a New Breed network gets going, I can pull from various places within that network and bring my best evangelists, some prophets, and some shepherds that can help build the team. Meanwhile, our teachers can throw day seminars to train the planting team about various things such as the role of the Holy Spirit, effective community outreach, or the biblical basis of church planting. It's the same principle as building a fantasy football team and picking the best of the draft picks to be on the ultimate dream team.

The more churches that are planted, the more people you pick up for the network. The groovy thing about this is that as the Mystery Machine rolls along to the next location, you get to hook up with people you don't know what you'd have done without. It's like Scooby Doo hooking up with Batman and Robin, or the Jetsons/Flintstones crossover. It's like the Avengers or the Justice League. When the network starts growing, you have some super-teams hooking up that can do greater damage for the kingdom.

Any skill you have can be used by the network. Eric Kirkough and Chris Duffy over at yourHost.com not only offered us dirt-cheap web streaming packages for all of our planters, but they also devised ways of hooking up poor planters with hardware to stream with. Calling his megachurches clients he said: "Hey, you know how you just upgraded your video equipment? What are you doing with your old equipment?" Usually, because megachurches have less time than money, the old equipment just sat around in a storage closet. Eric bought it cheap and reversed it to our planter at a steal. He'd never have gotten a deal like that on almost brand-new equipment, but that's how we roll because working like this will propel you further than you'd ever have gone before. Similarly, Pete Mitchell of Big Guns Marketing also started offering his talents to New Breed as a marketing guru, helping planters to generate support in ways they never thought possible.

But it gets better. At the time of writing this, I'm planting a New Breed Church Planting hub in Long Beach that will propel multiple

planters outward into the surrounding area. Because the hub isn't
dependent on me, I'll be freed up to help each planter as he launches
out. Like Paul, I've spied out hubs of influence from which to spiral
out in the surrounding counties. Because I'm mobile, we can spread
quickly first-century stylee.

MY WORK HERE IS DONE

Eventually, when the church needs to be able to stand on its own two
feet, God folds up the church planter like a Swiss Army Knife, so that
He can put him into His pocket and carry him to the next place his
skills are needed. Therefore, his most important task is to find guys
who can hold the bag once he's gone. John Wesley was noted for legendary administrative gifts when it came to moving his circuit-riding
preachers throughout the continent. His gift of administration was
such a loss to the movement that when he was promoted to glory, they
appointed a hundred men, known as the legal hundred, to take over
his role. The old saying holds true that you can tell the gauge of a ship
by the wake it leaves behind it. It took a hundred guys to coordinate
the Methodist circuit riders in the way that Wesley did. Like Wesley,
the apostle Paul was concerned that his wake didn't leave a gaping hole.

Check out Paul's emphasis in each of these scenarios and see if
you can detect a common thread:

- Paul and Barnabas went through Lystra, Iconium,
  and Antioch and "appointed elders for them in
  every church" (Acts 14:23).

- In Ephesus Timothy was instructed, "What you have heard from me in the presence of many witnesses entrust to faithful men who will be able to teach others also" (2 Tim. 2:2).
- Writing to Titus on Crete, Paul said, "This is why I left you in Crete, so that you might put what remained into order, and appoint elders in every town as I directed you" (Titus 1:5).

In every case of church planting, Paul was concerned with raising up local leadership to replace the Swiss Army Knife of the apostle. In each case, part of their instruction was to train others so that after they had tunneled deeply with the gospel, the support beams would support the work so there wouldn't be a cave-in when they pulled out. Furthermore, you can see the perpetual nature of the training: make sure you train others, who can train others, who can train others. When I first entered into the ministry, one of my mentors told me, "Your job is to work yourself out of a job."

Paul's method of ministry was to move in so that he could aim to move out. He would infiltrate a city, plant a church, train up leadership, and leave with some church-planting candidates trailing along. The apostle is a pair of needle-nosed pliers who gets in where nobody else can and then spreads himself wider and wide until he makes room for others to come in. Finally, he releases his grip and moves on, adjusting himself for penetration of tight spots again. Alan Hirsch called the apostle the "space maker."

An apostle has no problems taking the backseat and giving others opportunity. Like a mother bird, he pushes them out of the nest until they learn to spread their wings and soar. Then, when the Holy Spirit says something like, "Set apart for me Barnabas and Saul for the work to which I have called them" (Acts 13:2), the church is excited about the next church plant, rather than fixated on the leaving leader.

Handing off a church reminds me of the movie *Always* (which totally sucked, by the way), where a guy dies in a plane crash but "gets" to look on while his wife is being wined and dined by another dude after he's dead. On the one hand, he's happy that somebody's taking care of her, but on the other hand, that's still another dude kissing his wife. Or imagine painstakingly restoring a 1950s Chevy convertible, then handing it off to your sixteen-year-old son, knowing that he's probably going to scratch it up, forget to change the oil, and eventually crash it.

Painful, but it's the way the game is played. If the team is going to score a goal, you've got to be able to pass the ball, and letting go of a perfectly set-up pass isn't easy because you've got to have faith in the Wide Receiver.

Therefore, training up decent replacements is essential.

OTJT

Why is it that when a guy graduates seminary, the one thing he's ill equipped to do is most of the stuff that Paul did in Acts?

Think about it. If there was one thing you'd want to train guys to do, it'd be to plant churches.

Wouldn't you want to release dangerous delta force teams that were able to infiltrate, accomplish their mission, and then spread out to the next assignment? Instead, we have generations of guys who can navigate church politics, write blogs, drink coffee, and discuss the finer points of theology. The equivalent would be to ship a handful of commandos to a weapons depot for a couple of years and assign them to memorize the weapons specs and count the ammunition. Upon their release from "training" you wouldn't expect them to storm terrorist bunkers with any degree of success. Our men aren't dangerous.

How then did Paul put his leaders through boot camp? He took them with him. He planted churches and used them as training grounds to train up future planters like Timothy, Titus, and Silvanus. His methodology was watch, do, train:

1. I do, you watch.
2. You do, I watch.
3. I do, you do.
4. You do, you train.

Paul's OTJT (on-the-job training) was the most effective way to prepare guys for ministry. Jesus seemed to think so too. He did it with twelve guys for three years.

I spoke with a young guy who was serving on staff at his church. He was convinced that God was calling him to plant, and everything checked out. Even those in leadership at the church were convinced that he was called, but they kept telling him he wasn't ready. I was all ears.

Me: "How are they going to help train you so that you're ready?"

Future church planter: (long pause) "I don't know." (longer pause) "I don't think they know either."

I'm sure they didn't. Most churches don't. They'll tell a guy over and over that he's not ready to plant but won't release him to go train. In New Breed, the first thing we offer is on-the-job training. If you come to us and say you want to plant, after assessment we'll normally turn you over to a church plant currently going on and say, "Follow that guy and learn from him." It's the biblical model.

In Acts 13:4 Paul's missionary team was referred to as "the two of them" (NIV), yet by the time they sailed from Cyprus for Turkey in 13:13 it was "Paul and his companions." You could say that he was a pick-up artist! During his first drive-by church-planting journey across Cyprus and Turkey, Paul had a second agenda. He was creating future team members as he collected converts.

Planting churches, he left rows of newly converted seedlings whom he would later reap as future church planters as he swept through on his second visit. In the case of Timothy, Paul came back for him after he'd grown from a seedling into a sapling. The team swells, fluctuates, breaks off, and at times even splits. Paul's ministry in one location trained up fresh meat to take with him to the next location.

If I'm going to plant and I've been coaching you, then I might take you on some field trips. If I go to Long Beach to plant and you live within an hour's radius, I'll probably ask you to make the drive to join us so that you can learn on the job. Eventually, when you're ready, I'll send you out. I'll know when you're ready because I'm observing you as you increasingly step out and colabor with me in frontline gospel work.

William Arthur observed:

> When [God seeks] laborers, He goes not to the
> places we should have thought of, nor does He cast
> in the moulds we should call most becoming.…
> [T]he theory of the Methodists is that no train-
> ing for the work of God is like training in it; and
> that, however valuable study in preparation for the
> ministry may be, actual service is absolutely indis-
> pensable; and when that is voluntarily rendered, in
> such a way as to give full proof of call and qualifica-
> tion, it offers a certificate with which no other can
> be admitted into comparison.[4]

Similarly, Martyn Lloyd-Jones raised up a whole generation of preachers in twentieth-century Britain whom he affectionately called his "boys." I've been in close association with men he mentored, and I've been privileged to hear stories about phone calls that brought the Doctor to their doorstep within hours to help with whatever crisis they were dealing with in their young ministerial lives. There he would sit with them face-to-face as they poured their hearts out. He'd counsel them, and then back to London on a train he'd go. If the situation was untenable, he'd make arrangements through his extensive contacts for them to go somewhere else. Spurgeon, like-wise, had a pastor's college and gave generous amounts of time to it. Wesley, Whitefield, Booth, and others saw networking as crucial to reaching their generation, and the effects of their stones thrown in the pond are still rippling across the waters hundreds of years after they've gone.

Being dead, they still speak. Has the church been listening?

For too long the church has been producing young men content to hold ground instead of take ground. The church's command from Jesus was not to "hold till I return" but to "secure the beachhead" of every distant shore. Every time that God has sent His Spirit in power, a wave of pioneering daredevils has charged the gates of hell. The Lollards, Luther's missionary monks, Zinzendorf and the Moravians, Wesley and Whitefield, the Cambridge Seven, J. Hudson Taylor and the China Inland Mission, Bill Bright and Campus Crusade for Christ. Networking together for the gospel is something that the Spirit moved His missionaries to do in the New Testament and throughout church history, and I believe He is doing it again in this generation.

The stuff you read about in Acts and church history can only be learned on the front lines, not behind the desk in an air-conditioned office where you hope nobody will come in and interrupt your studies. You're not going to change the world hiding behind your desk.

So, what'll it be—beat cop or desk job?

Personally, after downloading all of this into your head, I'm hoping you have a Neo moment and say, "Whoa! I know kung fu!"

BLOWING UP THE DEATH STAR

Some indeed preach Christ from envy and rivalry.

Paul, Philippians 1:15

Everybody wants to pass as cats.
We all wanna be big big stars, but we all got different reasons for that.

Adam Duritz, Counting Crows, "Mr. Jones"

Today, I saw a man in town. People were throwing daisies at him
and giving him goodies. Sometimes I would like that kind of respect.

Nacho Libre, *Nacho Libre*

Luke: "Come with me. Leave everything behind."
Darth Vader: "Obi-Wan once thought as you do."

Return of the Jedi

THE RETURN OF THE JEDI

In the beginning of *Star Wars IV: A New Hope*, Luke is just a punk kid who blasts womp rats in his T-16 at home. They're no bigger than two meters.

In *The Empire Strikes Back*, he completes a little training and goes off half-cocked, thinking he can take Vader. He gets his arm chopped off.

In *Return of the Jedi* he … well, he returns. This time, he confronts his father, telling Vader that he can turn back to the light. Luke tries to persuade Anakin that he no longer needs to be a puppet of empire building.

I relate to Luke. When I went into ministry I was nineteen years old, had no training, and whined a lot. Then I raced across the globe to confront forces that were stronger than I am and got some butt-whuppins. Yet in the end I met some Yodas, saved some friends, and completed my training. Now I've returned home, and I see the American church that fathered me, and I know there is still good in it. I can feel it. In this chapter, I'm appealing to the Jedi that exists in every big church pastor out there in hopes that the warrior who first embarked on a mission to save the world will be reawakened within him. If that happens, it may result in danger to your position; it might be ministerial suicide; it could even destroy the Death Star construct that you've built. But maybe, just maybe, it will set in motion events that will save the galaxy.

You're gonna hate me for writing this chapter.

Nonetheless, I am a Jedi, like my father before me. I'm convinced that if we blow up the Death Star, the empire building will cease and kingdom building will go back to its rebel roots.

WARNING: THIS CHAPTER COULD BE HAZARDOUS

Matisse once wanted to burn down all of the art galleries and museums and start all over again. It didn't happen, but his "liberating color" has had a profound effect on how people see art.

My idea for church reform was once packing a time bomb underneath every empty church building and blowing our superstructures sky high so we'd have to start all over. Like construction workers say, "A new build is easier than a rebuild." There's only one problem with that. People. There are people in your churches for whom Christ bled, and we've got to take them with us.

Journalist Gloria Steinem once quipped that the truth will set you free, but first it will piss you off. She was right. There's still enough punk rock left in me that is pretty antiestablishment. I believe Jesus was the ultimate radical and often made religious people mad. My Celtic bones have been etched like scrimshaw with a serious streak of Welsh nonconformity. That is my tradition. I make no apology for it, but please understand that I'm writing this chapter because I *love* the church.

Most of the reformers started out thinking they wanted to reform the church, not leave it. And for the record, I'll never leave her. She birthed me, nurtured me, and made me what I am (did we both just shudder at that?). I owe Christ and His bride *everything*. I am grateful to the generation that went before me and held the torch so that my generation could see. Swindoll, Begg, Sproul, Smith, Laurie, Graham, Piper—all of these men inherited a system from the previous generation, and they faithfully held the torch for my generation. In no way am I criticizing these men to whom I owe so much. What I am criticizing is the system that holds us captive—the matrix of modern ministry. Like Morpheus, I'm hoping to unplug others from the chest tubes, flush them down the pipes, and set them free. Otherwise, you'll spend the rest of your days curled up in the fetal position in some red embryonic-fluid-filled pod, having all your battery juices sucked up by the big machine. I'd rather see a revolution in Zion.

After spending the past twelve years around blue-collar factory workers, steel and dock workers, roughnecks, and people who shot heroin for breakfast and met prostitutes for lunch, I'm a little rough around the edges. I'm definitely not sure if I'm ready for America yet, but should this book get buried in a time capsule and dug up twenty years from now, it's gonna make a whole heck of a lot of sense.

Get ready; I'm pulling the pin on the hand grenade and tossing it into your lap.

THE THINGS WE THINK AND DO NOT SAY

At the beginning of the film *Jerry Maguire*, Jerry is a cutthroat sports agent who hates his life. One sleepless night he has an epiphany about how things should be and writes a memo for his coworkers called "The Things We Think and Do Not Say." His radical manifesto costs him everything, and in his passion for what he believes, he commits himself to a vision. As a church planter I relate to that.

I admire the sea of faces that show up at our conferences. These people have faith to see something that doesn't exist yet and are brave enough to follow the vision. Jerry asks, "Who's coming with me?" He gets a secretary and a goldfish after his stand at the office. I'm still relating.

The tension in the film, as Jerry's life is crumbling, is that Cuba Gooding Jr. could walk at any minute, leaving Jerry with all that sacrifice and nothing to show for it. But Jerry's about to learn what makes somebody great, and it's not becoming a successful sports agent. Throughout the hardships in the movie, Jerry is forced to live out his manifesto, almost against his will. That's the purpose of this chapter—to challenge you to live the manifesto of your convictions.

I find it sad that two thousand years on from the church's birth, we still have to choose between playing it safe or being biblical. Yet church history teaches us that big corporate religion has always been on the wrong side of being biblical, from the Sanhedrin to the church during the civil rights movement. Martin Luther King Jr.'s "Letter Written from the Birmingham Jail" addresses the church's role in the American civil rights movement:

> There was a time when the church was very powerful.... Wherever the early Christians entered a town the people in power became disturbed and immediately sought to convict them for being "disturbers of the peace" and "outside agitators." ... Things are different now.... If today's church does not recapture the sacrificial spirit of the early church, it will lose its authenticity, forfeit the loyalty

of millions, and be dismissed as an irrelevant social
club with no meaning for the twentieth century.[1]

Being a biblical reformer got Jesus killed. From the day when He
sat in the sun weaving cords into a whip to upset the money chang-
ers' tables, He was a marked man. We've not even begun to approach
how radical Jesus was.

Jim Petersen, former vice president of The Navigators, listed
three basic approaches to change:

> There is change by revolution, change by reforma-
> tion, and change by innovation.
>
> Change by revolution is almost always more
> destructive than constructive. It is a revolt against
> the prevailing system. It seeks to put an end to that
> system and replace it with another....
>
> Reformation has to do with attempting to fix
> an existing system. It is change by reordering what
> is there....
>
> Change by innovation is accomplished as innova-
> tive people experiment and learn within the sphere of
> their own lives and ministries. As they learn through
> their experiences, others are able to pick up on
> what they are doing and carry the discovery process
> further.... It experiments and learns without impos-
> ing the discoveries on the rest. It does not insist that
> everyone and everything around it adopt the changes.
> It thus leaves what is already in existence intact.[2]

Planters are already out there innovating change through church planting as they follow the Spirit's lead. If things are going to change inside the church via reformation, then we're going to have to pay attention to some kingdom ethics that fly in the face of how big religion operates.

BUILDING THE KINGDOM, NOT EMPIRES

When you're in violation of kingdom ethics, the motorcycle cop of biblical truth will flash his lights and ask, "Do you know why I pulled you over?"

We smile innocently. "Why no, officer. I wasn't aware that I was breaking any laws. I thought I was just going with the flow of traffic."

The truth stares us down, and in the awkward silence we offer up a weak confession. "I suppose I was going a bit too fast. My mind must have been on something else."

The truth officer's jaw unhinges as he exclaims, "I didn't pull you over for your speed! I pulled you over because you were going the wrong direction on the freeway!"

The church has been going the wrong way for a couple of decades, and kingdom ethics have begun pulling us over. It's true that we've been speeding, roaring at breakneck speed, trying to fill our buildings with listeners and pouring all of our money back into our own pockets so that we can fill our next building with even more people (as soon as the next building project is done). Kingdom ethics were staring us in the face the whole time, but our minds were on something else.

Empire building.

Kingdom ethics make for bad empire building. If we're the Rebel Alliance, all of our X-Wings should be sporting a "No Empire" bumper sticker: a picture of the Death Star with a red circle slash through it. The focus shouldn't be cramming more people into our churches, but seeing more people rescued from the tyranny of Satan, sin, and self. If that means merging churches, halving churches, or—God forbid—helping other churches, then we'd gladly do it to see people rescued off the road to perdition. As a card-carrying member of the Rebel Alliance, I want to blow up the Death Star, because I believe it's hindering us from recognizing God's agenda.

Kingdom ethics such as "serve one another," "give to him who has nothing," and "throw a banquet for those who cannot repay you" serve as little packets of C4 that will blast away the flawed foundations of empire building. Do you like blowing stuff up? I sure do.

One of my favorite parts of *Saving Private Ryan* was when they took old socks, and filled them with bubble gum, gear grease, and explosives and made "sticky bombs" that they could attach to the wheels of the Tiger tanks. As the self-serving megachurch lumbers by, I'm gonna lob some sticky bombs at its wheels and see if I can knock the treads off. Otherwise, the unstoppable force may lumber on and deal more massive destruction to the cause of Christ.

There are three philosophies advancing the tank treads, and they are barriers to kingdom advancement: size, money, and personality. Hand me a sock.

SIZE AIN'T EVERYTHING

The reason I'm lobbing a sticky bomb at the size wheel is because of the assumption that bigger is better. Megachurch pastors slap the God-talk on the growth of their churches, claiming, "God blessed the work." I've heard that from guys I respect (and I believe that God has blessed some of them), but I've also heard it echo from false teachers. Come to think of it, I've heard it from everybody with a big church. Strange that nobody ever says that all this money and power has been a curse upon the work.

Is it always a blessing? I wonder.

There's nothing wrong with being big. Megachurch is *not* the enemy. In the New Testament, megachurches like Jerusalem, Antioch, and Ephesus became *sending agencies*. They supported church planting and launched repeated missionary journeys. Churches acting as sending agencies use their power and size to propel their members outward instead of unwillingly leaking them out to competing churches across the street with sexier programs. Functioning like Antioch, these megachurches fund teams who leave networks of church plants packed with fresh converts. The new blood nourishes the mothership as they serve the wider network and team up for evangelism.

I believe God is awakening many of the apostolic leaders currently running megachurches so that they will be driven to expand the kingdom. They are beginning to move their "best guys" where they are needed, and are themselves, like the apostle Paul, encouraging, sharing, visiting, and assisting the churches throughout their network. When this happens, leaders who've become like David, staying at home "when the kings go out to war," smell the thrill of battle again. Like King Theoden of *The Two Towers*, languishing on his throne at the mercy of Grima Wormtongue, they will rise up and regain the ability to pick up a sword, hacking against the tides of darkness. Like Caleb at eighty-five, they'll be ready to take on the giants again, feeling as strong as ever. They become gospel outriders, visiting new works, preaching in the frontline trenches primarily to the unchurched. God can use their honed gifts powerfully, as their guns produce battle smoke rather than simply languishing oiled, polished, and shiny in the barracks week after week.

During the Great Awakening in Wales, the Methodists established an apostolic network to further the kingdom of God. Their emphasis was on spreading out to the farthest corners of Wales and penetrating the heart of every village. Today, every village has the exoskeleton of an eighteenth-century chapel building to prove it. The eighteenth-century apostle, known as a circuit rider, usually got up at 4:00 a.m. and rode out before first light on horseback, preaching from town to hamlet to village. You might kid yourself that times were easier then, but those were the days when people climbed trees and urinated on you while you were preaching or physically dragged you to the cobblestones and kicked the snot out of you. To date, I've never had a face full of wee for preaching the gospel. Nonetheless, because of this apostolic ministry, the gospel spread.

Without diminishing the power of the Holy Spirit, we can say that the Great Awakening really was the great apostolic networking. These men were "content to work in small places with small resources, but huge potential."[3] So what happened? In Wales at least, after circuit riding for years, the men all settled down into local pastorates, lured by comfort and stability, and the outward momentum was lost.

Sound familiar?

FILTHY STINKIN' MAMMON

The second tank tread I'm targeting with my sticky exploding gum sock is money. Jesus pulled no punches when it came to finances and the kingdom. He once lamented that the sons of the world were wiser with their money than the sons of the kingdom. The church is raking in money by the millions but spending it all on itself, whereas kingdom principle dictates that if you have two cloaks and your brother has none, you should give one cloak to him. Instead, the church has more cloaks in the closet than Imelda Marcos had shoes. She once said, "I did not have three thousand pairs of shoes; I had one thousand and sixty." Glad we cleared that up.

In his book *Radical*, David Platt pointed out that America gives a billion dollars a year to missions. That sounds impressive at first, until you realize that America spends the same amount on chewing gum annually. One repentant pastor confessed that after scrutinizing his budget, on average their church had to spend millions of dollars on overhead before it could eke out one single buck for international missions. Because large churches often exist to keep the big machine going, we don't spend money on anything that does not first benefit the machine. Instead we simply create bigger staff teams to keep the Christians inside the church happy, thus fostering further introspection.

Assistant pastor, youth pastor, junior high pastor, marriage and family pastor, administrative pastor … And we get further and further from apostles, prophets, and evangelists. We couldn't afford to put them on staff if we did hold to that model. We're too busy prioritizing staff to babysit Christians so that they don't go somewhere else, taking their money with them.

According to *Leadership Journal*, nearly 40 percent of Christians still believe that evangelism should be a way to grow *their* church, rather than the church at large.[4] Somehow our decisions are measured in financial meetings by what they will do for the church itself. "Will we get a return for this investment?" I learned from many years of sitting in board meetings that everything eventually comes down to money.

Businessmen are great. They are great for strategizing about marketing and untangling financial knots, but they suck at leading churches, and I'll tell you why. It's because they take calculated risks based on one question: "If I take this risk, will it pay off?" The kingdom of God doesn't work like that. Jesus calls us to do things that don't pay off and frequently don't make sense. Ask the disciples about a crazy night of fishing when Jesus asked them to do something they *knew* wouldn't work: "Put out into the deep and let down your nets for a catch" (Luke 5:4). It went against their expertise, but "at your word I will let down the nets" (v. 5). They obeyed. It paid off. It still didn't make sense.

Apostolic teams should be funded by megachurches to venture beyond the barbed wire, out into no-man's-land, and start churches. Yet the way that things are now, the most effective office in Scripture for expanding the kingdom of God is not just unrecognized—these guys have to work menial jobs, scrape enough cash together to provide basic things for their church plants, and sweat day to day about where the funding will come from. When I think about the travesty of this, I unlace the kid gloves. If you don't see equipping the apostles and evangelists as more of a priority than building your private empire, then frankly, you don't deserve to be holding the office that you do.

I warned you this chapter might crack a few knuckles and split some noses, and I know I've ticked you off. But is it the truth? If so, it'll set you free from the straitjacket of an insane system. You may be thinking, "Who in Xanadu do you think you are to punch me in the nose?" Remember that faithful are the wounds of a friend, but deceitful the kisses of the enemy. I care. That's why I'm writing. As leaders we get too used to people kissing our butts so much because they want something from us. I want you to reform.

Reformers John the Baptist, Luther, John Knox, and Richard Baxter all busted a few ribs in their day. I think it'd have been cool if Richard Baxter wore Doc Martens like me, but he was dead before his country invented them. Nonetheless, if you need somebody with buckles on their shoes to validate what I'm getting at, listen to Richard Baxter in *The Reformed Pastor*. You'll quickly see why this book has fallen out of popularity with ministers today. Most people in our generation can't stomach it, but Baxter hailed from the Puritan age when spiritual giants walked the land, not this day of small things when dwarves sip lattes, doing what's right in their own eyes. Baxter made ministers man up. Criticizing ministers that lived on such large salaries when they could be using that money to spread the kingdom, Baxter challenged them to cut their own salaries and split their wages with gospel partners:

What! do you call yourselves ministers of the gospel, and yet are the souls of men so base in your eyes, that you had rather they should eternally perish, than that you and your family should live in a low and poor condition? Nay, should you not rather beg your bread, than put so great a matter as men's salvation upon a hazard, or disadvantage?—yea, as hazard the damnation of but one soul? O, sirs, it is a miserable thing when men study and talk of heaven and hell, and the fewness of the saved, and the difficulty of salvation, and be not all the while in good earnest. If you were, you could never surely stick at such matters as these, and let your people go down to hell, that you might live in higher style in this world.... Must I turn to my Bible to show a preacher where it is written, that a man's soul is worth more than a world,—much more therefore than a hundred pounds a year,—much more are many souls more worth? ... Or that it is inhuman cruelty to let souls go to hell, for fear my wife and children should fare somewhat the harder, or live at lower rates; when, according to God's ordinary way of working by means, I might do much to prevent their misery, if I would but a little displease my flesh, which all, who are Christ's, have cruci-fied with its lusts? ... Must not every Christian first ask, In what way may I most honour God with my substance? Do we not preach these things to our

people? Are they true as to them, and not as to us?
Yea more, is not the church-maintenance devoted,
in a special manner, to the service of God for the
church? And should we not then use it for the
utmost furtherance of that end? If any minister who
hath two hundred pounds a year can prove that a
hundred pounds of it may do God more service,
if it be laid out on himself, or wife and children,
than if it maintain one or two suitable assistants
to help forward the salvation of the flock, I shall
not presume to reprove his expenses; but where this
cannot be proved, let not the practice be justified.

And I must further say, that this poverty is not
so intolerable and dangerous a thing as it is pretended to be. If you have but food and raiment,
must you not therewith be content? and what would
you have more than that which may fit you for the
work of God? It is not "being clothed in purple and
fine linen, and faring sumptuously every day," that
is necessary for this end. "A man's life consisteth not
in the abundance of the things that he possesseth."
If your clothing be warm, and your food be wholesome, you may be as well supported by it to do God
service as if you had the fullest satisfaction to your
flesh. A patched coat may be warm, and bread and
water are wholesome food. He that wanteth not
these, hath but a poor excuse to make for hazarding
men's souls, that he may live on dainties.[5]

And how modern ministers love their dainties.

What would Paul say if he could see us enjoying the dainties of our pampered and pedicured ministries? "Wow, you are so blessed! I wish I could trade places with you!" I doubt it. Does it shock you that Paul sometimes didn't have money to eat, or buy clothes to replace the ones that were ripped off his back? Think of it. Paul was the most gifted man out there for expanding the kingdom, and only the Philippians would help him do it financially (Phil. 4:14–17). I have a feeling that there are many unsung heroes out there furthering the cause of the gospel in hard-bitten lands, and they worry from day to day how they're going to pay the bills. Meanwhile, we continue to repaint the sanctuary, upgrade our sound system, build bigger barns.

My heroes in ministry are the guys who'd love to be paid for what they do, and if they got paid at the value of how hard they actually work, we couldn't afford them. They embody one of my favorite quotes from Bob Shank: "Career is what you're paid for, but calling is what you're made for." I've been a bivocational planter for over ten years, and I dedicate this chapter to my bivocational brothers-in-arms in hopes that pastors with integrity will begin to recruit them onto their teams so that they can be freed up to run at it with everything they have.

I'M TOO SEXY FOR THIS PULPIT

The final sticky bomb made from my sock is lobbed at the celebrity performance element in our churches.

Today's generation are looking for leaders that they can follow. Before they can follow you, they need to know they can trust you, and you can be certain they don't want to help you build your megachurch. They're asking, "Are you for me, against me, or for yourself?" After all, the job pays well, provides awesome perks, and brings a certain degree of power and celebrity. They've learned from the church's modus operandi, which focuses on self-improvement, builds bigger barns, buys expensive toys, and has little time and energy for mission. They've watched their parents' generation approaching God like a consumer product, and they're not impressed.

When Francis Chan walks away from it all and infiltrates the Tenderloin district in San Francisco to minister to down-and-outs, people listen.

The issue in the modern church is that for too long we've bowed down at the altar of personality, serving the ego of our leaders. Church has become a place to go and witness the antics, wisdom, and giftedness of the pastor. The church settles down into the seats as an audience, ready for the big show. And anybody in show business will tell you that the better the crowd, the bigger the fame, the bolder the paycheck. Like Bono sang, "They put Jesus in show business, now it's hard to get in the door."[6]

The bottom line for teachers whose prime directive is to build crowds through entertainment is that they're worried they'll lose people, and we all know what that means:

Fewer people … less money. Less money equals … but wait, we've been there already.

Somehow we thought it was okay to take the *Nacho Libre* view of the ministry where we want people to throw daisies at us and give us goodies.

It all comes down to this operating principle: we've gotta keep 'em by playing to the crowds and entertaining the masses with clever homilies, or they'll leave. They've already begun to leave—we just haven't been paying attention. As a result of the valuable time, attention, and resources wasted on empire building over the last two decades, church planters are now having to reclaim the defecting prodigals while expanding the kingdom outward. The late great Larry Norman once challenged America that it had starved its children to beat the Russians to the moon. Our churches got to the moon, but where are the youth? I realize this is a tough pill to swallow, but I've witnessed it with my own eyes. When I left this country in 1999, the youth were still around. Now we're lucky if we can keep the church kids. Research says that 90 percent of them end up leaving after watching our shenanigans.

There is coming a time when the parents are going to ask the spiritual leaders in this country some blunt, serious, and difficult questions: why did our kids leave? Why didn't you address it? Why didn't you stop it? Of course, the churches will lay blame at the feet of the parents and say that it started at home, but the parents will respond, "You were supposed to be leading us as we led our families." The fact is, we didn't give a rip about their families—just crowds. Getting more families to the drive-thru window of our churches just meant that we got to supersize our order.

And today's youth see right through us. They see our big buildings as moneymaking machines raking in millions of dollars, and they're disgusted. In the book *The Millennials*, an unchurched girl named Rebecca said, "The Boomers give money to the church, but it comes right back to them to keep them content. They hire the staff to do the ministry they won't do…. That's not New Testament Christianity. That's a religious social club."[7]

Some pastors have been playing the game for so long that they feel unable to leave their pulpits for too long to help new gospel initiatives because the church has become a personality cult about them. Because they don't occasionally share the pulpit with four other roles, people demand that Pinocchio dance for them every Sunday, and as long as people keep throwing the gold coins onstage, they keep dancing. Sadly, if they'd discipled others, they would have been expendable like Paul, with an apostolic backup team at their disposal. Paul could leave a church at a moment's notice, as he had to in the case of Thessalonica and other churches he planted.

If there isn't an arsenal of discipled guys waiting to take to the skies to plant and others to hold the fort down, it's because the leader has neglected his duty to train up men who are also able to teach others. When the church fixes its eyes upon leaders as the Corinthians did—"'I follow Paul,' or 'I follow Apollos,' or 'I follow Cephas'" (1 Cor. 1:12)—it's taken its eyes off of the crucified Christ. It's unbiblical for leaders to allow it and carnal to enjoy it. When Corinth became enamored with personalities, Paul's antidote to Satan's snakebite was to administer the anti-venom of looking to Jesus "crucified for you" (v. 13). When people get their eyes focused back on Jesus and the cross, it eliminates most of our problems in Churchianity.

I've got a theory that if you attempted church reform, you'd lose about 90 percent of your people. That's why most pastors will never do it. Good riddance, I say—let their butts darken somebody else's pews as they exercise the gift of sitting. If you unloaded the burden of the dead wood, as in Jesus's pruning illustration, you'd really begin to channel sap into the concentrated areas where it would create greater fruitfulness.

Back when I was a nurse, I dealt with burn wounds. There is a growth of scar tissue known as eschar that forms over severe burns. Although eschar seems to be healing, it means that the healthy tissue underneath can't breathe and therefore can't heal. So one of the difficult things nurses get to do is debride the wound. That's a fancy term for "rip that sucker off." It hurts; people yell, cuss, scream, and pass out. But it's done so that the tissue will grow healthy, and, my friend, that's the only way to ensure that you're going to grow a healthy church atmosphere.

It's time that somebody stood up, broke the glass, and sounded the alarm, unafraid that it might interrupt the show. Shouting fire in a movie theater isn't popular, but it's necessary when there's a fire in the projection room. I'm alarmed, and you should be too. Jesus basically told His disciples, "Be alarmed when all men love you" (Matt. 10:22). As Admiral Akbar cried out in *The Empire Strikes Back*, "It's a trap!" Satan's motive is to keep you from spreading yourself out, handing over to others so that they can grow, and playing your part in expanding the kingdom of God!

It's like he's taken us to the highest mountain and promised to give us "all of this" if we'd only bow down and serve him. In "Vertigo," Bono paraphrases this passage: "All of this / All of this can be yours / Just give me what I want, and no one gets hurt."[8] We've been giving the Devil exactly what he wants in return for "all of this." But by serving our own ambitions and idols of "success," we've compromised the mission. Jesus wouldn't take the shortcut but chose the way of the cross, serving others, laying down His life so that others may find theirs.

What about us?

Chris McCandless went out into the wild and spent years exploring the vast spaces of North America. He wrote his elderly friend Ron,

> So many people live within unhappy circumstances and yet will not take the initiative to change their situation because they are conditioned to a life of security, conformity, and conservatism, all of which may appear to give one peace of mind, but in reality nothing is more damaging to the adventurous spirit within a man than a secure future. The very basic core of a man's living spirit is his passion for adventure.... [Y]ou must lose your inclination for monotonous security and adopt a helter-skelter style of life that will at first appear to be crazy. But once you become accustomed to such a life you will see its full meaning and its incredible beauty.... I fear you will follow this same inclination in the future and thus fail to discover all the wonderful things that God has placed around us to discover.[9]

What would you give if you could leave it all behind and start all over again?

A question that we frequently ask leaders when taking part in church revitalization analysis is, "If you could do it all over again, would you do it differently?" The answer is always yes. The next question we ask is, "Then why are you still doing it the same way now?"

The honest answer is you know how much it would rock the boat and empty the seats.

Am I buggin' ya yet? Don't mean to bug ya.

ANGER AS A CATALYST

I'm actually trying to make you a little angry. Angry enough to make you want to change.

Call it angst; call it anger; call it frustration. Call it whatever you want. Every revolution begins with the buildup of frustration that bursts apart and floods the world with radical action.

Take Rosa Parks. For her whole life, Rosa Parks had been sitting in the back of a segregated public bus. But on Thursday, December 1, 1955, in downtown Montgomery, Alabama, when she was tired and exhausted after a hard day working at the Montgomery Fair department store, something happened on the Cleveland Avenue bus.

She got angry. She'd had enough. And the dam burst. The anger, frustration, and angst of black Americans like Martin Luther King Jr. broke into peaceful demonstrations in the form of the Montgomery Bus Boycott. Although peaceful, the powerful revolution of unstoppable force was under way in America.

The list of people goes on: Judas Maccabeus, George Washington, Martin Luther, Gandhi. All of them were propelled into action by the buildup of a fire in their bones for liberation, justice, or truth.

Powerful stuff, anger. A God-given emotion that has a reason. It's a motivator, a catalyst. I learned years ago that if I'm not angry enough about something, I usually do nothing. I don't fill out that customer complaint form or write corporate headquarters. I won't write my congressman or protest at the polls.

Over the past few years as I've coached church planters, I've noticed that they all have this one thing in common. In assessing their calling, I usually ask them what is the chief thing they're feeling. Almost all of them answer, "I'm feeling frustrated." I don't mean a sour, churlish kind of frustration that causes them to backbite and murmur against leadership. I mean a holy frustration.

Like caged animals, they can't wait to be let loose upon a lost world with the gospel. They were made to be flung far and wide, and as with a catapult, the more you hold them back, the tauter the tension cable gets until they become damage dealers in the realm of the Spirit when they're finally released.

Holy frustration.

Paul had it. Here was a guy who'd trained for ministry at the feet of the finest his entire life, only to have his ambitions dashed by Jesus.

Back to Tarsus.

Back to tent making.

Back to obscurity.

For twelve-plus years Paul sat plying his family trade, mumbling, "I coulda been somebody, Johnny! I coulda been a contenda!" And as he sat stitching skins together, the fire in his bones smoldered. Year by year, Paul's passion for the revelation of the gospel grew with the pressure of a geyser as predictable as Old Faithful.

After Barnabas's fist rapped at his door a decade later, Paul never slowed down, never looked back, and never quit. Like the Energizer Bunny he kept going, wearing out young men and eating hirelings for breakfast. The only way God could slow him down enough to get him to write Bible books was to lock him up. The only way to get him to stop was to decapitate him.

Whitefield had this holy frustration. Not content to confine the gospel within the four walls of the church, he literally took it to the streets, fields, coal mines, and frontiers of America, exclaiming, "All the world is my pulpit!"

Remember William Carey sitting in that cobbler shop, staring up at the map of Asia, frustrated that the passage to India was so difficult? Wringing his hands in agony, he exclaimed to bewildered students during geography lessons that "there are millions of them there! Millions! And they're perishing without ever hearing the gospel of Christ!" His work as the Father of Modern Missions started the day another "missions" meeting was ending in inactivity. On May 30, 1792, the association of ministers concerned about world evangelization sat for another meeting wherein nothing but talking about the problem occurred. As all arose to leave, Carey turned to Andrew Fuller in despair and tragically asked, "Is there nothing again going to be done, sir?"[10]

Even after being told, "Sit down, young man! If a sovereign God wants to convert the heathen, he doesn't need *you* to do it," by superior clergyman John Ryland, Carey's resolve was not deterred.[11]

That day, frustration turned to anger. And in the providence of God, something popped.

There are millions going to hell, and statistical evidence points to the numbers increasing with every passing year. I pray you'd be angry enough to do something about it.

At the end of just another year of regrets, Woody Guthrie sat down and penned his famous "New Year's Rulin's." There were thirty-two in all, but the last three are application enough to all that we've said so far:

> 30. Love everybody.
> 31. Make up your mind.
> 32. Wake up and fight!

The question is, do we love everybody enough to make up our mind, wake up and fight? When discussing the hold that the Matrix has on people, Morpheus tells Neo, "You have to understand, most of these people are not ready to be unplugged. And many of them are so inured, so hopelessly dependent on the system, that they will fight to protect it."

THE CONCLUSION OF THE MATTER

Wow, you made it this far. Well done. I didn't think that most people would.

Jesus, Paul, Luther, Calvin, Wesley, Whitefield, and Spurgeon were all radicals. If they were alive today, we'd write girly rants about them on Facebook. But Spurgeon's dead, and a dead Spurgeon is a safe Spurgeon. He can do no harm from the grave, so we write nice things about him … but most churches in America wouldn't want these guys as their pastors. I've written this chapter in hopes that there are more Luthers, Wesleys, Whitefields, Spurgeons, and Lloyd-Joneses alive out there who will reemerge as radicals in our time. They've been as rare as Jedi in the Original Trilogy; either hiding in deserts or swamps like Ben and Yoda, or exterminated by Order 66.

After reading this chapter you may think that I've made this journey to the Death Star only to strike you down. The truth is, I've come on a mission of love to save the Anakin Skywalker lost beneath that black samurai armor and breathing apparatus. I sense that there is still good in most pastors. You were once good Jedi, and the force of the Holy Spirit once flowed strong through you. I want you to stand before the Lord and still be able to hold your place among glowing blue dudes.

It's not too late.

I feel the conflict within you. Don't tell me, "It's too late for me, son."

You can reject the messenger all you like. Just don't reject the message. Strike me down, because I will not turn. I am a nonconformist like my fathers before me. Strike me down, or grab the emperor and throw him down the energy shaft, and free countless millions from the empire agenda.

The choice is yours.

8

WHY YOUR
CHURCH SUCKS

*To the Jews I became as a Jew, in order to win Jews.… To those
outside the law I became as one outside the law.… I have become
all things to all people, that by all means I might save some.*

Paul, 1 Corinthians 9:20–22,

*Among the many reasons assignable for the sad decay of true
Christianity, perhaps the neglecting to assemble ourselves
together in religious societies, may not be one of the least.*

George Whitefield, "The Necessity and Benefits of Religious Society"

*I went to your schools, I went to your churches, I
went to your institutional learning facilities …
so how can you tell me that I'M crazy?!?!*

Suicidal Tendencies, "Institutionalized"

It's your kids, Marty—something's gotta be done about your kids!

Doc, *Back to the Future*

This Sunday morning, I want you to engage in a sociological experiment. Turn your head to the left, then swing it to the right. Take mental stock of the average age of the people you see. Do you notice those middle-aged, graying people? How many teens and young adults do you see?

We've lost the youth. Young people think our churches suck, and they've voted with their feet. The youth exodus has begun.

In Britain, this happened during the cultural revolution of the 1960s. Nobody was alarmed. In fact, they hardly noticed because the crowds were still big. When the older generation started dying off in the next twenty years, the churches started shrinking. As everyone panicked, they awoke to a twenty- to thirty-year generation gap, and the tired, silver-haired souls were too old to do anything about it.

I have good news and bad news.

First, the bad news: it's happening now, and because our numbers are still swelled, we're not alarmed. After speaking at a conference, I commented to my wife, "America isn't ready yet for what we're saying. It's like they have to be where Europe is before they'll wake up." The alarm is set to go off in about ten years. Meanwhile, just keep hitting the snooze button. Until the plane is in a nosedive, people can't be bothered to think of their seats as a flotation device.

Statistically one in four young adults claims no religious affiliation, and the number of youth who've left our churches is around the 90 percent mark. They've sat in our pews, scribbled in our Sunday schools, swayed to our worship, and then left. What happened?

Resistance to change is what got us here. Our "modern" worship is just one of many symptoms of our reluctance to move forward. Let's face it: most of our contemporary worship is still stuck in the 1980s. If worship is really cutting edge, it sounds like a U2 rip-off, but youth don't listen to U2. We sing U2 rip-offs because we like them; therefore, we don't change.

To what degree are we willing to sacrifice the next generation to preserve our little brand of church?

But it's not style of worship that's keeping them away from church. It's not even evangelical truth. It's the style of our life. When people are asked why they don't come to church anymore, they list these five reasons: church is irrelevant, legalistic, hypocritical, too political, and filled with self-righteous people. Gandhi once remarked to E. Stanley Jones, "If Christians would really live according to the teachings of Christ, as found in the Bible, all of India would be Christian today."[1] Perhaps Jesus isn't irrelevant as much as the church is.

ALONE TOGETHER

Ed Stetzer points out that 86 percent of unchurched people say that they can have a good relationship with God without belonging to a church.[2]

Before you have a defensive knee-jerk reaction to that, I want you to think of *why* they're saying it.

Perhaps you've overheard someone saying the following, "I don't need to go to church. I can still have a relationship with God at home. If I want to listen to a sermon, I'll download something from the Internet. If I want to worship, I'll hit my favorites off of iTunes. I'm not really missing out on anything by staying at home. Watch the show at church, or watch it at home. What's the difference?"

How do you answer that?

Do you tell him he should go because the presence of God is there and he'll miss it? I'll tell you what he'll say: "Why wouldn't the Holy Spirit meet with me just because I wasn't physically sitting in the building? I can spectate just like anybody else from the comfort of my own home. I can be blessed in the worship, and get edified from the Word, and save gas all at the same time."

Of course, you'll be quick to talk about Hebrews 10:25—"Don't forsake the gathering of the saints together," you'll say—and he'll be quick to respond with, "Well, I do meet with other Christians for coffee like we're meeting now. We're talking about Jesus." But the truth is, he's getting more fellowship with you speaking into his life to get him to church than he will in church. He definitely won't starve from the lack of chitchat he'd get drinking coffee after the service, with the few people who actually stick around instead of burning rubber during the final song. You might even answer that he needs pastoral leadership, but we've already established that he's not really going to get pastoral care at most of our churches. Unless he can fit into the pastor's schedule, or he's lucky enough to have penetrated the iron curtain of secretaries and receptionists, he'll never see the great and powerful Oz.

As long as the church is set up as an audience on a Sunday morning, there's little to say to the departing youth. There's nowhere for them to get involved. They sit at home in the neon light of their monitors because all they need in church is ears, eyeballs, and legs. All we ever ask them to do is sit. We never ask them to use their mouths.

And they've got so much to say.

ME THE MEDIA

This is the media generation. Before they've graduated junior high, they're already making their own movies on their computers. If I'm googling tutorials on how to use the latest version of Photoshop, I'm usually sitting there feeling like a complete moron while listening to the wisdom of some thirteen-year-old punk kid unfolding the boundless mysteries of the Adobe universe. This generation grew up and the Internet was already there from day one, while most of us can remember the technological revolution as it happened.

Blogs, YouTube, Facebook, Twitter. Everybody has something to say. They don't care if it's important, polished, or relevant. They've just got to say it. If they like a product, they blog about it. If they are watching TV, they participate in the show's online chat. Music, food, clothing, and everything else provides a link, a space, an opportunity to be heard.

Then they walk through the doors of a church, and we tell them to sit down and shut up. Listen to us! Quietly! If you want to talk about it, wait until the event is over, and talk about it when you get outside—because we don't provide anywhere to do that sort of thing.

This is where we're blowing it. As usual the church will be decades behind the cultural revolution for fear that it might be compromising, but missionaries study a culture and find the "in" for the gospel. There's never been a way more conducive to the gospel than giving the lost an opportunity to feed back into what they've heard. The most unchurched generation during my lifetime, the blog generation, has unwittingly provided the church with the tools to reach them, and this is where the church, if *it* were willing to sit and listen quietly, could learn a lot. This generation not only will give us the keys to unlocking dialogue with them, but may teach us how to be more like the first-century church.

I get the impression from reading the New Testament that church was a participatory sport, and this generation doesn't want to be spectators.

Are you beginning to understand why they think your church sucks?

THE GOSPEL ACCORDING TO [FILL IN THE BLANK]

This current generation will demand that we rethink how we preach the gospel. Testimonies have always been a powerful tool, but they make this generation weak in the knees like kryptonite can make a bullet penetrate Superman's chest. This generation wants to hear other people's experiences, and testimonies are like shotguns in hillbilly country. Everybody has one.

What is the gospel according to you? How was Jesus good news to your life? You've got a story to tell, and this generation has been hardwired by pluralism to listen. For generations now, the church has bemoaned pluralism as if it made the lost any more lost. Unbelief is unbelief, no matter what clown shoes it wears. The Holy Spirit still saves people all the same, and they will still find their hearts melting under the power and person of Jesus Christ. Pluralism has unwittingly done something for the church. It has provided us with an open doorway of evangelism. Paul was able to share Jesus in Athens, because a pluralistic society craved new thoughts and experiences in a pick-your-part-religion. You see, a pluralistic society has to value every opinion to remain consistent. Although pluralistic societies are less responsive to propositional truth, they are far more open to subjective truth.

Please understand that I'm not in any way advocating a departure from preaching objective truth. As Lloyd-Jones frequently pointed out, if we do that, we fall into the enemy's hands. They will explain us away with psychology, assigning us a portion with J-dubs, Mormons, and Star Trek nerds who believe Romulans are real. We must continually ground our experience in objective, historic bedrock, and preach it stronger than ever.

But in the book of Acts, Paul's testimony is written in full three entire times. Get that. Luke didn't just write it out once in Acts 9 and then reference it later with a footnote—"see chapter nine to catch the gist of what Paul told Agrippa." No, to the mob in Jerusalem and Agrippa both, it is unfolded again in varying detail (Acts 22; 26).

Parchment, vellum, or whatever Luke wrote on was expensive, it was time consuming to rewrite the same facts, and I'm sure Luke's hand was getting tired. So what was the Holy Spirit trying to tell us by recording it thrice? That in a pluralistic, pagan society, your testimony is so powerful that it can't be heard enough! It's so hardwired into postmoderns that they can't argue with "your truth" or "your experience." While pluralism may have trivialized evangelical dogmatism, it's simultaneously opened another door for the Spirit to work. While you're sharing your testimony, lace in the propositional truths that the Holy Spirit used to change your heart, quoting Scripture at every turn. Your testimony is a secret weapon in today's society. If they attack your testimony, then challenge them on it, ask them why they can't accept it if they believe that all personal experiences are valid. It's fun.

Incorporating one person to share his or her testimony for five minutes is a way that the entire church can be used to proclaim Christ.

SYNAGOGUE STYLE VERSUS PROCLAMATION STYLE

There's another way we can use this cultural tendency to take us nearer to the first-century church. As a missionary Paul said that he became all things to all men, to reach them. As a master missionary, he'd learned to adapt to the culture. Nobody had to change as dramatically as Paul when converting to Christ. Up till his thirties, Pharisee Paul had been stuck in the rut of tradition, but God commissioned him to set others free from their prisons, and the most radical thing he was ever called to do was eat a hot dog. Pork belly, pork ribs, pork roast, pork chops, fricasseed pork, pig skins, you name it. Paul became a porker for Jesus.

Jesus loved those pagan porkers, and Paul didn't have to be asked twice to eat the candy of meats. His customs, routines, and personal preferences changed so that he could bring the gospel to the Gentile world. You can actually trace this in Acts. When Paul went to Athens, he used the Greek means of communication: proclamation. At the Areopagus, Paul was perceived as a babbler for Jesus as he sang loud and proud about the resurrection. But when he went into the synagogue in Corinth, he sat down rabbinical style and presented his teaching in a blend of teaching mixed with discussion as he reasoned with Jews and sympathetic Greeks in the synagogue (Acts 18:4). And the Corinthian church was born.

I'm convinced that if Paul were here today, he'd opt for the synagogue-style approach to reach the millennial blog generation, because with all their blogs, tweets, and review posting, this generation is hardwired for interaction with the gospel.

Search your feelings; you know it to be true.

I would in no way advocate lessening the length of preaching, unless your sermons are boring, but I would say it's sheer lunacy for us to merely preach at people rather than blend the proclamation style with a synagogue style. Synagogue style is interactive, and the modern generation wants to contribute. I suggest preaching your normal sermon and then providing discussion immediately after.

I've lost you, haven't I?

THE WORLD NEEDS GOD AND GOOD COFFEE

It all started in a Starbucks, by accident. I'd been working as a barista in a huge Starbucks in Borders Books (may they rest in peace). I'd been asked about *The Da Vinci Code* so many times that I decided to start a reading/discussion group about it for "one night only." Thirty unchurched people turned up. At the end of the night, they said, "Can we do that again?" When I asked them why, the response floored me, "We were able to drink coffee, ask questions about Jesus, and nobody yelled at us." Did you get that? They wanted to come back and talk about Jesus some more because we showed them respect.

The most evangelistic book in the Bible, John's gospel, is filled with conversations between Jesus and other people. It's not a bunch of sermons that Jesus preached, but a record of discussions. There's a reason why people connect so much with it. Discussion raises the questions of those who don't believe and gets to their obstacles to and excuses about faith. When you listen to what they have to say, the Spirit will guide you into applying the Word of God based on their questions, struggles, and dilemmas.

Why then is discussion or a chance to contribute not given in our churches? Why aren't we seizing upon this cultural phenomenon and harnessing it for the gospel? If this generation can't be a part of what's going on, they will switch off, tune out, and drop off.

Shouldn't they be central to what we're doing?

In the UK a phenomenon called the Alpha course took Britain by storm. It started off with a meal that was prepared by the hosts, then after the small talk over dinner, the dishes would be cleared away and the host would present a few questions that were open for discussion, such as "Why don't people believe there is a God?" Then there was a forty-minute video in which a guy named Nicky Gumbel masterfully presented the gospel. This was followed by a time of open discussion that lasted about forty minutes. It was powerful. Churches that hadn't seen conversions in decades began to launch the ten-week course, resulting in professions of faith.

The only problem was what to do with them afterward. When the new converts went to the Sunday services they found the experience nothing like the approach that had connected with them in the first place. They were asked to sit down, shut up, and listen—quietly.

And for this generation, that sucks.

CHURCH IN A BLENDER

What happens when Starbucks, A.A., and church are put in a blender? For one thing, it makes for a longer church service.

Have you ever been to an A.A. meeting? If not, you really need to go to one. Everybody shows up because they know that they're screwed up. That's more than you could say for most churches. People who drag themselves into A.A. know that if they had it all together, they wouldn't need to be there. That's how church ought to kick off every week. It's not about being good, but about being screwed up and needing Jesus. What they go there for is to be around other people who are struggling with the same things and receive encouragement. Sound familiar? Alcoholics Anonymous perfectly sets the tone for how church participants ought to relate to each other as they go to a place because they need each other's support. The philosophy is, "If I don't have you in my life, I'll suffer." If I wasn't screwed up by sin and in need of Jesus, I wouldn't be here.

When you go to A.A. you get to interact. When you go to Starbucks, you get to talk. But our services are wired in such a way that people have no opportunity to do anything but sit back and enjoy the show. If we hotwired church to be all about participation, we'd really have something, though. A.A. knows that people need to talk about their dark and dirties. Starbucks got the nickname "fourbucks" because it can charge you four dollars for a cup of coffee for offering something a diner doesn't. Interactive atmosphere. Starbucks is set up for participation, and that's the key.

To this end, Whitefield and Wesley had a plan after they blew through towns and left a wake of converts. Rather than leave the newbies like shepherdless sheep, they formed "societies"; interactive home fellowships structured for discussion, prayer, and Communion. That's what converted the Great Awakening from an evangelistic campaign into a movement. Incidentally, it's also what the early church did when they met from house to house following Pentecost.

REARRANGING THE FURNITURE

The Puritans believed that how you set up the furniture of the church room preached a nonverbal sermon. Prior to the Reformation, the altar had center stage and communicated that you needed the priest to mediate between you and God. The Reformers scrapped the altar and placed the pulpit at the center of the room to emphasize the centrality of God's Word. The only other furniture in the room was chairs or pews set in straight rows, but what *that* communicated to people was that they were an audience. What a mistake!

When you read the New Testament, you can see that people prayed for one another, sang songs spontaneously, engaged in the activity of Communion, brought words of encouragement to one another, and responded to prophecy, among other things.

Even the Old Testament temple worship was participatory. It was not an audience-based affair. You went to the temple with something that you yourself either raised or bought, and you handed it over to the priest to slay, so its blood sprayed all over you. You weren't an audience, but a participatory player contributing in a blood sport, like a tourist sitting in the first eight rows at Sea World but getting splashed with blood instead of water. It was God's way of saying, "You're a part of this." Likewise, in Communion, I am actively participating in something when I eat the bread and drink the wine. I'm saying, "I'm a part of this. It was my sins on that cross."

In order for interaction to occur, we've got to set church up for participation. When I accidentally planted out of Starbucks, we sat around in half circles. Circles communicate participation. Facing each other tells you that you're going to be a part of what happens here. Your contribution matters. It's not just welcome, but expected. Now, let me ask you something stupid. If that's not being communicated by the way you do things, how do you expect real fellowship to happen? Or discipleship? What about evangelism? Give me a good reason why that shouldn't happen on Sunday. Because of numbers? So, in effect, we've sacrificed quality for quantity.

Typical.

How will your people use the gifts like encouragement and compassion? Ironically, the one thing that doesn't tend to happen on Sundays is fellowship. Christians shuffle in, watch the show, and then elbow each other during the death race to blow the holy popsicle stand. No wonder our youth stay at home. Nobody is going to listen to their problems. If anybody talks to them at all, chances are that nobody is going to ask them anything meaningful beyond "how's school?" All of our after-service talk is so trivial, I'm convinced that we don't even know what real fellowship looks like.

Picture a church where you walk in the door and there are eleven groups of coffee tables with eight chairs in a half circle around them. The horseshoe-shaped grouping is facing the screen for worship and preaching, but you get the sense that you're not going to just be able to blend into the crowd. Taking a deep breath, you make your way to the table. You are nervous, but here's the beauty of it. Everybody at the table you walk up to is so relaxed and smiling and talking. You hear people laughing, and somebody in your group asks you if you'd like to have coffee or tea. With a cup of coffee in your hand you start to relax when somebody asks you what your name is and offers theirs. You get the small talk out of the way until the worship starts. You sing. In between the songs, a couple of people share a Scripture, somebody shares a prophesy, a couple of people pray. Finally the sexiest man in the world comes up to preach—just kidding, it's not Pillar or Refuge; it's your church.

After the preaching, three simple yet searching open-ended questions are presented on the screen. Coffee, tea, and cakes have mysteriously arrived onto your table during the post-preaching song, and you're eager to talk about some of the thought-provoking, con-victing, and encouraging things you've heard. As you talk with the people you quickly realize that everybody else is as human as you are.

They struggle, just like you. They get impatient with their kids, just like you. They get afraid and unsure of themselves, just like you. The difference is that they keep leaning on God, and after listening to them, you conclude that He seems to be helping them.

So you've got your coffee tables, you've brewed your coffee, and you have your logo emblazoned on your mugs. You're all set, right? Not exactly. It's not as easy as it sounds. I need to warn you that if this is going to work, there are a few basic principles. Most importantly, there needs to be a group leader to prevent absolute chaos and steer the group while not hogging it. The key is to let the nonbelievers in your midst talk. For example, the question might be, "What do you think heaven is like?" If a Christian answered, "He is encinctured with an auriferous zodiac" (as one of Spurgeon's students at the Bible College once answered, trying to impress him), it would intimidate and confuse everybody and probably kill the group. Therefore, it is important for Christians to be humble, patient, and tolerant.

It takes a mature believer to be able to handle somebody coming in and whizzing on your electric fence by saying, "I believe that Jesus was a space alien, and one day He's coming back to take us onboard the mothership." We all know that's the wrong answer, yet it would be a huge mistake to break out the Bible like it was our S-Mart twelve-guage double-barreled Remington shotgun. We often come off like Ash from the Housewares department when we wield the Bible like a boomstick and address them like they were the Army of Darkness: "Listen up, you primitive heathen savages." Instead, you have an opportunity to be like Jesus.

Sit by the well, have some coffee, and talk with them about Him.

THIS GENERATION CRIES OUT

This generation is crying out for love connection, and I don't mean Chuck Woolery. The Internet seems to connect us, but only in a trivial way. People are becoming less authentic in their communication. They can now watch a girl cut herself to the bone and yet be unable to help her in any way. The reaction of most in the pixilated spectator e-arena is to mock, or troll crass comments, because they've been desensitized. It's their only choice, as their ability to act compassionately has been stripped away by the glass barrier of their monitor. In the area of conflict, things aren't much different. People are now able to say things that they wouldn't dare say face-to-face because the Internet provides little or no accountability. What's inadvertently created is an illusion of fellowship in a virtual community.

As I survey the cultural shift of recent years, I hear my heart echo Jesus's parable: "an enemy has done this" (Matt. 13:28). There is a demonic agenda to keep us from talking face-to-face by giving us a false sense of connectedness in a virtual society. Genesis demonstrates that man was made as a relational being. It was not good for man to be alone, yet since man's fall, man's disconnectedness from man has been the direct result of his inability to connect with his Maker, leading to a spiritual disconnectedness from himself and all others. Yet, according to Genesis, that can't give us what real community can. Man is still hiding, but this time it's not behind a bush but behind a computer screen. He's still ashamed, and the Internet takes away much of the social pressure. Pseudo-intimacy in a cyber community will sabotage interpersonal relationships, and from the Enemy's point of view, that's ideal. If the gospel is anything, it's a social animal. It takes root through community and interpersonal communication.

You don't just share an opinion; you share your life.

The theological way to say this is that true ministry is incarnational. If this wasn't true, then Jesus wouldn't have come in person. He'd have been content to share His opinion through the spoken and written word. But true ministry is always done face-to-face. Jesus, who took on flesh, was proof of that, embodying the word that He'd spoken long ago by the prophets. Jesus literally fleshed out the ideas spoken by the prophets because, as good as the words were, they weren't the same as being face-to-face. Paul said this repeatedly: "we endeavored the more eagerly and with great desire to see you face to face" (1 Thess. 2:17); "For I long to see you … that we may be mutually encouraged by each other's faith" (Rom. 1:11–12).

The one thing that this generation is crying out for is found only one place on earth: the church of the incarnational God. So incarnational is He, that He's not content to have a relationship outside of you, but has come to indwell you and incarnate Himself within your daily lives. The Holy Spirit indwelling you provides an intimacy unlike any other on planet earth. It's the only thing that will truly meet the soul's cry for intimacy, and love, and acceptance. It's found in community, where Jesus is lived out through the failure of others as they live and forgive. And there in the midst of us together, He promises He'll be there in a unique way.

Coldplay wrote, "Don't want to see another generation drop. I'd rather be a comma, than a full stop."[3] A full stop is the British way of saying a "period" at the end of a sentence. Is that what the church has become to this generation? I don't want to let another generation drop through the cracks because I was too busy "playing church." I want the Holy Spirit to so fill the church that, like Paul said, fear comes upon the people because they realize that "God is in your midst."

I've seen the Promised Land.

Returning to America after twelve years in Wales was the equivalent of stepping off a time machine from the future. Because Europe is decades down the dark path of post-Christendom, ministering there was like ministering thirty years into America's future. Now that I've returned I feel like Biff Tannen holding the 2015 Almanac in 1955. Returning to the biblical principles laid down in the book is all that's going to alter the future timeline.

Don't worry, I'm not going to start knocking on your forehead, saying, "Hello, McFly," or calling you a butthead.

GIFT-DRIVEN MINISTRY

If the whole body were an eye, where would be the sense of hearing?
If the whole body were an ear, where would be the sense of smell?

Paul, 1 Corinthians 12:17

If I thought I could win one more soul to the Lord by walking on
my head and playing the tambourine with my toes, I'd learn how!

William Booth

Don't ask yourself what the world needs. Ask yourself
what makes you come alive, and go do that, because what
the world needs is people who have come alive.

Howard Thurman

Tick: You know, Arthur, when evil is afoot, and you don't have any
arms, you've gotta use your head. And when evil is ahead and you're
behind, you've gotta do the legwork. But when you can't get a leg up,
you gotta be hip. You gotta keep your chin up, and kick some—

Arthur: Tick, we get the idea.

Tick, 1994

COME A LITTLE CLOSER

There's another reason we can give to the punk kid who asks why he should go to church. Two words: spiritual gifts.

If they were in operation on a regular basis, he'd never ask that question.

Let's face it: there are certain things that can't be done well over the Internet, like kissing. And there are certain things that only happen around the Thanksgiving table. Mom's hugs; Dad's proud, reassuring pat on the shoulder; the dog's slipping a little tongue into your nostril as you bend down. You have to be physically present for that expression of love. Delivery of the news, "You're going to be a father," "Will you marry me?" and "I regret to inform you that your son was killed in the line of duty while bravely serving his country" should not be communicated by texting.

So with spiritual gifts. The first-century church used their spiritual gifts during the service. They had to be told not to overuse their spiritual gifts. We don't even know whether or not we have any.

Paul established that spiritual gifts only operate when we're in the presence of one another: "For I long to see you, that I may impart to you some spiritual gift to strengthen you—that is, that we may be mutually encouraged by each other's faith" (Rom. 1:11–12). Nothing magical will happen as you sit there in church as part of an audience, but something supernatural *will* happen as you get involved in another person's life and through the gifts function as Jesus's hands, feet, and mouth. Jesus Himself will begin to interact with somebody through you as you serve that person through your spiritual gifts. Now that's something worth dragging yourself out of bed for on a Sunday morning.

Getting ministered to, but more importantly, ministering to others is epic for the interactive mind-set of this generation.

I FEEL SO USED

As a youth pastor, when I took a kid and forced him to save all his money, get onto an airplane, and fly to some foreign country, he came back supercharged for Jesus. What made the difference? He was using his gifts. The mission field allows you to use your gifts. Sundays don't. If Sundays were turned into the mission, he'd be given the same opportunity to supercharge his soul, but if you want him to sit down and shut up, he'll tune out and walk away. Mission is where he experienced the power of God channeling through him. Like the disciples returning from their mission into the hill towns of Judea (Matt. 10), he'll return revved up about what he saw and heard God do through him.

When the church becomes a theater, the attendees become an audience. They become spectators. The challenge of any pastor is when he tries to get an audience to start acting like missionaries. Somebody once said, "Christians are like manure. If you put them in a heap for too long, they begin to stink. But if you spread them out, they fertilize and become fruitful." Why? Because they stop being an audience and become missionaries.

In the early church, prophecy, encouragement, and the other gifts were allowed to function as people ministered to one another, and those gifts revealed the presence of God to unbelievers (1 Cor. 14:25). If I don't allow breaks in my service, then I don't allow God to break in. Nobody can share during the praise and worship time if they feel they're interrupting the performer's set. As E. Stanley Jones explained,

> The very setup of the ordinary church tends to produce the anonymous. The congregation is supposed to be silent and receptive, and the pastor is supposed to be outgoing and aggressive. That produces by its very makeup the spectator and the participant. By its very makeup it produces the recessive, the ingrown, the non-contributive, and the parasite. Men and women who during the week are molders of opinion, directors of large concerns, directors of destinies are expected to be putty on Sunday, and are supposed to like it. They have little responsibility, hence make little response, except, perhaps, "I enjoyed your sermon." They have little to do, hence they do little.[1]

The new breed of church creates opportunities for people to interact with each other. Small groups are hardwired into our service at Refuge Long Beach with the express intention of allowing people to minister to each other and interact with lost people. That's why coffee tables and horseshoes of chairs set around them are crucial. Nobody will get involved with the back of another person's head. Whoever thought that church should have people sit in rows was a moron. Greeting somebody next to you is just to allow the worship team to get the heck off the stage and allow the pastor to get his mic rigged up.

You can't truly fellowship during this time. I want to take the time to hear about the woman whose heart is breaking for her son who is in prison yet again. Nobody notices her in a big church, but in a small group, that woman is guaranteed to come week in and week out and have people listen to her, pray for her, and maybe even follow up by writing to her son.

The beauty of it is that all believers at that table have been given opportunity to testify about the grace of God in their lives evangelistically. Not only have believers used their gifts during the service, but there's also room for interaction with the newcomer to go beyond the four walls of the church by inviting them out.

GRACE FINDS BEAUTY IN EVERYTHING

Refuge Long Beach, where I'm planting, is an urban plant in the city's downtown area. We meet in a community center in Bixby Park. Every holiday weekend, the hall is unavailable because it's a government building. For this reason, every couple of months we have to meet outside with lawn chairs. Taking Matthew 10 as a text, we shocked our team one day by gathering them around like Jesus did the seventy-two and telling them that the teaching for the day was to go to the lost sheep of Long Beach and proclaim the good news of the kingdom. At first they looked stumped, but slowly they began to move out in pairs. Like the seventy-two, they came back rejoicing that incredible things had happened. Conversations lasted three hours, people broke down and wept, the hungry were fed, new friendships were kindled. Weeks and months later we are still witnessing the reaping of the fruit of that day.

Here is the letter I wrote to my planting team after that hard day's planting:

> By now you've begun to realize that church planting is not a spectator sport. It's a full-contact sporting event. You're going to sweat. It's going to hurt. You're going to get muddy.
>
> Yesterday, at Bixby Park, I saw you guys seeking and saving the lost.... I saw you leaving the ninety-nine to go after the one. I saw you sweeping the house for the lost coin. I saw you unloading some Jesus-style kung fu in the spiritual realm.
>
> "For the Son of Man came eating and drinking." That was Jesus's description of His own ministry. He was up close and personal, across the table and available, in your face and ready to serve. Simply put, He was available.
>
> "For the Son of Man did not come to be served, but to serve, and to give his life a ransom for many."
>
> I think that many of you are beginning to realize that you actually matter at Refuge Long Beach, and more importantly, to the kingdom. In a church plant, when you don't come, you leave a gaping hole. When you don't give, we're poor. When you don't reach out to others, the lost don't get reached.

Can you imagine what would happen if every once in a while, the average pastor pulled one of these on a congregation when they turned up?

"What? No teaching? No lesson? No worship?"

"Here is the lesson: teach what you've learned. Freely you've received, now freely give."

I imagine that we'd see a lot more people fired up for the gospel than we've ever seen before as the people of God step out in faith and actually begin to engage the community around them on a Sunday morning.

Now there's a thought.

If church has become a spectator sport, then we need to challenge people to get out onto the field. That's all great, but nobody would dare leave the bleachers and hop onto the field unless they were drafted onto the team. E. Stanley Jones spoke about leaders as coaches, equipping the saints to do the work of the ministry:

> If the laity only listen they will produce only listeners, but no leaders. If the pastors are the coaches of a team they will produce players. Out of those players they will produce coaches. Out of our present setup is produced increasingly empty pews. If the church is pastor centered, then the output will be rhetoric; if it is lay-centered, then the output will be action. It will be the Word became flesh instead of the word became word.[2]

But people have to know their gifts.

FIND YOUR PASSION

I don't ask Christians what their gifts are. Over the years, I've learned that most believers who've sat in traditional churches aren't just unaware of their gifts—they didn't even know they had any. They've never been called upon to use them. Ironically, they weren't required for what we call church.

Here is the secret to finding people's spiritual gifts. You don't start by looking for their gifts. You root around for what they're passionate about; and people are passionate about things that burden them. If you can track what a person's burdened for, you'll discover their passion. When you discover their passion, their gifts will be trailing along behind.

What I've learned to do is grab some local papers and throw them down in front of the small groups. I ask them to circle the headlines that tug on their heartstrings, identifying needs in the community.

Next, I ask them to dream big. I'm actually looking for their gifts, but they don't know that yet. I ask them to circle with a red marker a couple of needs that stand out to them from the newspaper and come up with a strategy of how to meet those needs. The rules are simple: their plan can't be limited by lack of human or financial resources. When they begin to dream, their passion starts to bubble to the surface, and I start to see what gets them excited. Then I discern what God created them to do when we were "created in Christ Jesus for good works, which God prepared beforehand, that we should walk in them" (Eph. 2:10).

This is the single most effective way to motivate a church to use their gifts. Here's why.

Following a business model, a pastor drafts his five-year plan. Shine everybody else; the pastor is the visionary with the secret-service earpiece, communicating with the president. Here's the problem; if you're the only one who gets to listen on the Batphone to the Commissioner, everybody else will stop answering it. Nonetheless, the pastor with the five-year plan draws a straight line out of a chalk-board that eventually breaks at various stages into multiple lines indicating growth in the programs, benchmarks, and goals he'd like to see. Now the people become a means to that end. So he cracks the whip over them, for more money to realize the vision. He pumps them for "more bricks, less straw." He begs, he weeps, he beats them until they become like the Pod People from Jim Henson's *The Dark Crystal*, mindlessly slaving with soulless eyes for the vision set before them. They've been steamrolled, and their passions have been buried under your five-year plan.

Rather than trying to get people motivated to meet needs that they don't give a rip about, I let their passions steer the direction of the church, knowing that the Holy Spirit has deposited a gift there. It's my job to ensure that they have a platform to use it. When God deposited our spiritual gifts to us during our salvation, a passion was kindled in our hearts about something we wanted to do for God; but somewhere, somebody down the line told us it was stupid, they weren't qualified, or it wasn't "the vision of this church." And something in them wilted as they tried to diffuse some of that energy by doing church chores. I've learned to sniff out people's gifts. Somebody animatedly telling me an elaborate strategy for meeting the needs of the homeless has the gift of helps. Somebody who wants to counsel and provide support for single mothers dealing with life's daily struggles in all shapes and forms has the gift of compassion.

And you can never predict who's going to be burdened for what.

Are you recovering huge amounts of addicts who need somebody to reach down into the gutter and pull them out? You're going to find somebody on your team has the gift of compassion and giving. If not, then somebody will turn up. Perhaps it's more accurate to say that God, in His providence, will supply what is lacking as every part of the body does its share. Heard that somewhere before too.

A friend and former coworker turned up at our church with the gifts of giving and compassion. A successful entrepreneur, he sat in the emergency room with our addicts as they detoxed, turned up at their apartments, cooked them food, and wiped vomit off the floor. He supported our church plant from the start, and his kids came to the church and got saved when we launched, but he didn't turn up to the church until he was needed. At the time, none of us were aware of the need, yet God knew that it was right around the corner and moved somebody strategically into that slot to fit it.

There's an anonymous poem that is liberating:

> I'm only one,
> but I am one.
> I can't do everything,
> but I can do something.
> And I will not allow the everything that I can't do
> to stop me from doing the something that I can do.
> I'm only one,
> but I am one.

WHEELS WITHIN WHEELS

I've learned that above all, people are what Jesus is concerned about. He's more concerned about what He can do *in* a person who serves than what He can do *through* that person. Quite frankly, He doesn't need us.

Besides, the world out there has way more needs than I, you, or any number of Christians can possibly meet. Therefore, my strategy is to let the gifts of the people in front of me drive our mission. Because the strategy starts with people's gifts, it therefore ends with everybody's involvement.

For example, if I've started with ten planters on my team, I draw a circle representing our church. Within that circle I place ten dots representing my team members. Next I draw a bigger outer circle representing our mission field. I then draw arrows from the team members' dots leading outside the circle of the church and into the mission field. Those arrows represent the direction their gifts will take us. Depending on the burdens, passions, and gifts represented by my team, those arrows could be anything from art exhibitions, to drug counseling, to a talking heads group in the local hipster coffeehouse. It may be that I've got an uncanny amount of artsy people. Then again, I might have a third of my church (which I do) made up of ex-cons and the recovery crowd. Those two tribes live on from different planets. I shudder to think of artsy hipsters attempting to style themselves to reach convicts, or my recovery crew walking into an art gallery. Getting people engaged on the right mission is crucial. Like a compass, they'll find their true North if you give them room to wiggle on the dial.

When we let the gifts determine the direction of the arrows, we may get some converts. For example, if five people get saved as a result of us strategically using our gifts, I draw five dots representing the new converts in our mission field. Next, I erase the small circle representing our church, and draw it bigger to encircle the five newbies.

Now the outer circle becomes our church.

Now we've got five new sets of gifts added to our original ten. The last step is to find out what gifts the new converts have and draw arrows pointing to an even bigger outer circle. Rinse and repeat as your church grows. If I have three gifted musicians with a heart to hit the city's stages, or three ex-cons with a desire to hit the barstools together and witness, or two film students who want to start a film club and critique movies, then I get behind them all, enabling them to weave the gospel into all of those activities as we engage our city on mission together. I just keep drawing arrows. The more I'm drawing dots, circles, and arrows, the happier I am as an apostle.

It's liberating when you don't have to do all the work but can sit in a corner doodling. When people ask what I do, I can either respond, "I do what Paul did," or I can say, "I draw pictures all day!"

My teachers were wrong … it did pay off!

10

FLAME ON!

For our God is a consuming fire.

Hebrews 12:29

I just set myself on fire, and people come from
miles around to watch me burn.

John Wesley

Set me alight … I'll punch a hole right through the night!

Bono, "In God's Country"

As for me, I say my prayers
then I just light myself on fire
and I walk out on the wire once again.

Adam Duritz, Counting Crows, "Goodnight Elizabeth"

Flame on!

Johnny Storm (*Fantastic Four*)

DOUSING YOURSELF WITH GASOLINE

In the sixties, Buddhist monks began pouring gasoline on themselves and burning themselves alive as a way of protesting the war in Vietnam. I've often looked at those photographs or film clips and thought, "Man, that guy felt pretty strongly about that." Well, he'd kinda have to, wouldn't he?

How strongly do you really feel about the gospel? Strong enough to douse yourself with kerosene and light the match? I doubt it. You wouldn't have the moxie to do it in the physical realm if you weren't doing it in the spiritual realm.

I want to tell you how to douse yourself with petrol so that you know how to be consumed by the fire of the Holy Spirit. Only He can ignite the spark, but there are a few ways to ensure that you're doused in gasoline.

This generation doesn't just want to hear your ideas. They need to see power. A pastor friend once told me, God convicted him for telling his congregation that they were an Acts 2 church. God asked him, "When were you ever an Acts 1 church?" In Acts 1, they sought the face of God for power—"Power will come from on high. Then you will be my witnesses" (v. 8, author's paraphrase). Power is not going to be an optional extra in the future like it has been for so long in so many churches. When things go belly up like they did in Europe, powerless churches won't survive.

Remember Acts 2 when the tongues of flame appeared above the heads of the apostles? We already talked about the fact that fire spreads, and that it was a great symbol for what was about to happen as they were empowered to take the gospel into the pagan world. But fire has another property that I believe God was trying to communicate.

Fire consumes.

Everything.

As a firefighter, I never did see fire stop consuming, sit back, and sigh like Mr. Creosote, "I couldn't eat another bite." Fire will consume everything in its path until there is nothing left to consume.

It will take it *all*, or it isn't fire.

Fire is an accurate picture of God. God's jealousy for our affections makes Him "a consuming fire" (Heb. 12:29). Because fire is just another type of energy, it needs fuel in order to burn. The trick, therefore, is learning what is good fuel for it to consume. One of the most stubborn fires to put out is a burning pile of old tires. We usually had to use suffocating foam to put out that stuff. That's how I want to be—fuel that is hard to extinguish because it burns so strong.

That's what happened in the early church. Those fire toupees on the heads of the apostles weren't there to cover their bald spots; they were symbolic of power that was igniting within the fuel of their lives. How long has it been since a fire burned so deep in you that nobody could quench the zeal that blazed in your soul? You were a fiery torch, blazing the glory of Jesus Christ, so that your witness was one of power! People walked away from you not quite sure what had happened to them. They'd had an encounter with the burning bush—God engulfing you in flames, yet you weren't burnt up. Only, they knew that the ground they'd just stood upon was holy.

If I've lost you, then you've got some cool experiences in front of you. Trust me, you've only touched the tip of the iceberg of Christianity. You may be about to change occupations from cleaning the backside of sheep on the back side of the desert, to beginning to lead God's people in dynamic ways.

In periods of revival, God sends His fire down upon His people, empowering them so that the gospel spreads like wildfire throughout the nations. Years ago, as a college student, I read countless books on revival and was so moved in my own soul that I kept looking to the church to see it happen. After receiving countless puzzled looks after trying to share my burden, I realized it wasn't going to happen in my church. I was in advanced microbiology at the time, and so I decided to start an experiment. Just like a cultured agar dish, I sought to see what would happen if I really went for it with God, no strings attached. My agar dish caught fire.

Now that would be bad in a science class but gets top marks in your spiritual life. I sought the Lord every morning for a couple of hours and then prayed in the afternoons for revival as I drove from Huntington Beach to Hermosa Beach and back. As I drove in my old VW up the 405 freeway, I begged God to send a consuming fire that would ignite our love and passion for Jesus. I started fasting on Sundays and setting the whole day aside to read through Lloyd-Jones's eight-volume commentary on Ephesians. I was eighteen years old. In front of the fireplace of my living room, with a cup of vanilla almond tea in one hand and the Word of God in the other, I started to learn how to go on a date with God. Just me, the Doctor, the Republic of Tea, and God.

A fire was lit in the hearth of my soul that burned hotter than the fireplace. My experiment worked. I sought the Spirit of God with all my heart, found Him, and was filled. It was personal revival. Revival might not have been raging outside me, or around me, but my soul wouldn't be satisfied with that excuse. In the spirit of Moses who pitched his tent away from the camp, crying desperately to God, "Show me Your glory!" I wanted to see His glory so badly that I didn't care who came with me. I had gone it alone, but I didn't stay alone for long.

Because fire spreads.

It spread through George Whitefield after the day he flung himself on his bed in desperation and cried out, "I thirst!" The Spirit flooded his room and soul, and Whitefield surrendered and was consumed by a hot holy heavenly fire. At the moment that the Holy Spirit rushed in, he laughed that it had all been so simple and cried out, "Joy, joy, unspeakable, even joy that was full of, and big with glory!"[1] At that moment, Whitefield became a spiritual millionaire. When he spoke, it was out of an experience of a satisfied soul, nourished from a well that sprang up within him into everlasting life. Not only that—it spilled out over the rim of the well of his heart and created streams of living water that others used to quench their thirst.

The Holy Spirit wants to well up within you so deeply that you never thirst again. Whitefield was a spiritual millionaire who made others rich, yet many of us are spiritual paupers. We live on PB-and-J sandwiches when God has prepared prime rib with garlic mash, piping hot and waiting at the table. It's not His fault if we refuse to pull up a chair and feast, or raise the overflowing cup and drink deeply from the wells of salvation. The well is deep, but we have no bucket.

This generation knows so little of these things that it's almost like finding disciples of John wandering around in Acts 19 who say, "We have not even heard that there is a Holy Spirit" (v. 2). Because of the shallowness of our experiences, we lack power in our public ministry. As one man said, "Perhaps we say so little because we have so little to say." The preaching of Whitefield was experiential. He knew the influence of the Holy Spirit in his life and preached deep yet solid stuff. It was deep theology, but it was theology on fire!

And that fire spread.

It consumed him straight out of heaven and continued to consume all that lay before him in an unstoppable wave of flame as the Great Awakening swept eighteenth-century America.

MEANWHILE, BACK AT THE RANCH

Paul wrote in Ephesians 5:18 about being filled with the Spirit. He was writing to third-generation Christians (grandkids to the original believers in Ephesus). They'd grown a bit stale, and their witness was somewhat lackluster. But he wanted them to know that there is more to Christianity than what they were experiencing. Have you ever wondered if there is something more?

Paul communicated to the Ephesians by using the temple as an illustration. They knew temples. The temple of Diana of the Ephesians was one of the seven wonders of the ancient world. Paul said that they were the New Testament version of the gold-clad temple of Jerusalem (easily a candidate for the eighth wonder of the ancient world). He got on his knees to pray that they "may be filled with all the fullness of God" (3:19)! Whew! That's a tall order, partner! But was Paul for real? You betcha! He even said, "Now to him who is able to do far more abundantly than all that we ask or think, according to the power at work within us, to him be glory in the church and in Christ Jesus throughout all generations, forever and ever" (vv. 20–21). That was Paul's way of saying, "Yeah, I was serious. Don't limit what God can do by your own experience. He'll blow your mind apart with the reality of what we're talking about here." Realize that when Paul was speaking of being filled with the Spirit, he meant business.

This is what is commonly called unction, and not many people believe in it anymore. Many people in ministry take Han Solo's preference for a trusty blaster at their side, rather than trusting in some ancient, hokey religion. Yet it is such a powerful force—those who have rejected it continue to bore the people who hear them. Not only that, but they fail to witness what God can do with someone set on fire.

Bring back the days where Spurgeon, testing the acoustics in the apparently empty Surrey Gardens Music Hall, cleared his throat and bellowed, "Behold the Lamb of God who takes away the sin of the world!" and an elderly repairman fixing one of the folding chairs on the balcony immediately fell under conviction of the Holy Spirit and placed his faith in Christ.

GAME ON!

You wanna hear a skull kicker? Church planting is the closest you're ever going to come to the book of Acts. There are two solid biblical reasons for this.

First, that's primarily what they were doing in Acts. Second, when you step out in faith to glorify Jesus and cross the barbed wire into no-man's-land, the Holy Spirit turns up! That's what Acts demonstrates repeatedly, and when anybody steps out on a short-term mission, it's like crossing over into the realm of the supernatural. Suddenly it's game on, and the things you've only read about in Acts and biographies start taking place. When you step out in faith to reach the lost, you're planting the cross in enemy territory like it's a flagpole, and it's the Holy Spirit's job to honor that.

Over the past ten years, fourteen out of fifteen churches that have grown significantly have done so by transfer growth. That means that church hopping, pew jumping, and sheep stealing accounts for over 90 percent of our church "growth." Church plants are the one out of fifteen that are growing chiefly by conversion. They stepped out, and the Holy Spirit is turning up—big-time. Jesus promised His presence to perpetually be wherever missions are: "I am with you always, to the end of the age" (Matt. 28:20). That's a unique promise for the Holy Spirit to be with us in mission, and He'll attach Himself to anyone who wants to glorify, magnify, and superfly Christ.

Jesus said of the Holy Spirit, "He will glorify me" (John 16:14). Everything He does is with that one aim in mind. Not surprisingly, the Christian shares that same exact job description with the Spirit. To glorify Christ is the sole reason that the Christian is left behind on planet earth. Therefore, when the Holy Spirit sees somebody who makes it his or her business to magnify Christ, He forks His lightning down to that sucker like a lightning rod. You might say that the Holy Spirit is looking for somebody who will align himself and his purposes with the purposes of Christ.

In central California there are huge windmill turbines erected with the intention of harnessing the power of the wind. They have to be strategically placed, or their big propeller blades won't budge an inch. If they don't catch some wind, they'll just sit there and cost you tax dollars. Therefore, somebody somewhere had to know where the wind blows to know where to sink the windmills so that they'd generate power. Places with hills and valleys form natural wind tunnels. That's the kind of spot you want. Likewise, if you want to know where a spiritual wind tunnel is, you have to know where the Spirit is likely to turn up. The wind can't be tamed; it blows where it pleases. But I'll tell you where it pleases. Anywhere somebody is yearning to glorify Christ and step out in faith will find the roaring wind of the Holy Spirit at his or her back.

SOMETHING STINKS

I've been concerned that the Holy Spirit is a much-neglected topic in current church-planting discussions. As if we could do it without Him.

Therein lies the rub for self-sufficient America. After traveling all over the world a bit, I've concluded that Americans excel in personal hygiene, but I'll tell you where we stink. It's in thinking we can run church without God.

Let me be very clear about this. You can grow a church very big without the Holy Spirit. False teachers do it all the time. But you can't manufacture His holy presence. You can't generate a single conversion without Him or spark a fire that consumes the lost in its path for years to come. That's revival, and all men who have been at the center of it have had challenging things to say about the Holy Spirit. He was personal to them. They were in awe of Him, didn't fully understand Him, but always gave Him the credit for the tsunami of the Spirit that picked them up and carried them, destroying or saving everything in its path.

Until you see buildings, cars, trains, and freeways being carried along by a tsunami, you don't realize that such things are even possible. If you read a book about revival, you'd be tempted to think that people were simply making things up. In today's ecclesiastical configuration, we've taken the Holy Spirit out of the equation, and it just doesn't add up. Rees Howells said of the 1904 revival, "We had that same joy in the Revival, in the knowledge of a Risen Christ and the assurance of eternal life—unspeakable joy—but at the same time we felt the lack of power for service."[2] One of Wesley's circuit riders once remarked, that he had "seen him bring a drunken sinner to tears by a single sentence."[3] That's power!

It's easy to do church without God. But there's so much of man in it, and so little of the presence of Jesus. Jesus said He'd be there when two or more are gathered; do you know why? I think it's because He wanted us to know that serious things happen in prayer, and it only takes two people to get serious. Sometimes it's just the power of one. But the power of one backed by One is an unstoppable army.

David said, "In your strength I can crush an army; with my God I can scale any wall" (Ps. 18:29 NLT). And he should know. What the armies of Israel couldn't do, one faith-infused teenager did as he ran screaming at a giant with the wind howling at his back.

Sometimes the silence is deafening. The absence of the Holy Spirit in our discussions on church planting in books and blogs has in many cases broken my heart. I'm not an unbiblical, laugh-in-the-Spirit, slay-you-sucka, wack-job either. I'm simply a guy who knows that Spurgeon marched to his pulpit absorbed in his own thoughts, trembling with fear, but repeating over and over the reassuring words, "I believe in the Holy Spirit, I believe in the Holy Spirit, I believe …"

It's not just in our silences either. It's in what we say. James rebuked the first-century Christians for speaking about their lives like God didn't exist. We talk the same lingo. Recently, I was reading a book on church-planting leadership teams. One of the suggested steps of building a leadership team was, "Ask yourself who would be the best fit for the job."

Did you catch that? Ask yourself.

I'm not one to grill a guy over semantics, but that's as far as it went. There was no mention at all of praying for the Lord to reveal who those right people were. It was simply "ask yourself." We've been asking ourselves for far too long, when we should have been on our faces before God. Jesus stayed up all night praying before choosing the Twelve. There are seminars on leadership, conferences about building effective teams, but nobody talks of praying and fasting—asking God. How far we've fallen.

Even the Son of God asked his Father. But we ask ourselves.

Methodist minister William Bramwell once said, "Too much conversation with the world, too much preaching and hearing, and too little self-examination and prayer.… It is astonishing how the devil is cheating us, and at the same time filling our heads, and emptying our hearts."[4]

Of course, this is the pattern the church has followed throughout history. When small and insignificant, the church seeks power from on high to reach pagan, epicurean, godless cultures. However, every time the church becomes large and prosperous, it tumbles into spiritual famine. Following Constantine, the church went into decline, yet the Dark Ages brought a resurgence of apostolic movements among the rampages of pagan tribes across Western Europe. When Europe became more stable and prosperous in the High Middle Ages, the Roman church was able to centralize power, and that led to the abuses the Reformers opposed. During the growth of the Victorian Age, liberalism was introduced, and with it the rise of higher criticism. And now today.

I suppose it's no different in our personal lives. When we begin to prosper, God takes the backseat. Like the church, we rest on our laurels and kick into our default setting of do-it-yourself. Like the Israelites in the book of Judges, we've chucked God behind our backs, telling Him, "It's cool, God, we've got it now. Thanks for the help, but we'll take it from here." And the cycle repeats—until the next pagan invasion.

Enter postmodernism.

I once read a quote that said we stripped Christianity of the supernatural, and the lifeless husk that was left over was no longer worth believing in.

THE CYCLE OF DESPAIR

Okay, you were wondering when I was going to get back to the statistics. Every church-planting book has them. Including this one.

Here you go:

- 3500 churches will close this year.[5]
- Eighteen percent of America's 300+ million people go to church. Eighty-two percent don't. Doing finger math tells us that 250 million people in this country are unchurched.[6]

We need God again, and the world's bringing us to our knees. Face it—they're killing us. Although the current situation is merely the redux of first-century paganism, being brought to our knees is what actually gets us to fall on our knees. Once the compromise with the world brings churches to near extinction again, they'll finally look up and cry out in desperation for God to save them. This applies to theology as well as practice. If our church dial is set at self-reliance, it seeps into our theology. Legalism and reliance upon our own devotions and efforts replace real Christianity, which looks to Jesus alone. In many churches today, Christians know so little of the gospel, they could be said to be grace illiterate. In every case in which the Spirit of God has worked powerfully, there has been an emphasis upon the grace of God and the atoning work of Christ on the cross. The connection between the grace of God and the outpouring of the Spirit is not coincidental. It is in the theology of grace alone that Christ is exalted higher than man's feeble efforts. The Spirit rushes in to magnify Christ in a gospel that assures "a debtor to mercy alone, of covenant mercy I sing."[7]

Likewise, in practice there is no need for the Spirit if I can continue to fatten the self-perpetuating machine by simply showing up and preaching. How do we know if the Lord is still turning up? We assure ourselves that in the "two or more" passage He promised to turn up, but do we even allow the possibility that Jesus may not like what He sees when He gets there? Could the eyes that blaze fire be scrutinizing our self-aggrandizement? Is it feasible that He would have some critical things to say to us as He did to the seven churches of Asia? Are we humble enough to turn to God and ask, "How long, O Lord? For You no longer go out with our armies."

It reminds me of a joke: a man took a fancy to a church notorious for its exclusiveness. He told the minister he wanted to join. The minister sought to evade the issue by suggesting that the man reflect more carefully on it and pray for guidance. The following day the man told the minister, "I prayed, sir, and the Lord asked me what church I wanted to join. When I told Him it was yours, He laughed and said, 'You can't get in there. I've been trying to get into that church for ten years Myself, and have been unsuccessful.'"

When I started church planting, I noticed the difference between the way I had been doing ministry and the way that God worked. I thought it was downright decent of God to let me tag along. God turned up. It was like going from a cheap screwdriver to a DeWalt industrial power tool. The right tool makes all the difference, but this one is indispensable.

When He turns up, stuff happens that you can't control, imitate, or fabricate. Here are just a few highlights of the early days of my first church plant where the Holy Spirit turned up:

We printed up leaflets with a flyer that was designed to grab the attention of unchurched Brits. One day we all set out to distribute them through people's mailboxes. Once we'd finished the neighborhoods, we still had tons of cards left over. My wife had the idea of going to get some coffee at Starbucks and then distributing them onto parked cars. I was like, "No way! We don't want to start off by being annoying," but everybody else thought it was a great idea, so I went along. There I was, a bit like Jonah, hating every minute of what I was doing, when I heard a voice say, "Hey, what kind of rubbish are you putting on my car?"

Turning around, I half expected to see an angry rugby player ready to put me into the hospital again, but this time it was somebody I knew. I'd been window cleaning to make ends meet, and Nigel was one of my customers. He didn't know God yet, but he said, "You want to know something really weird? We were just talking about you, coming out of the grocery store. We were discussing whether we should go to your new church, and then we looked up and you were literally putting a leaflet under our windshield at that very moment!" He was laughing out loud and saying, "I'm an agnostic, but that has to be God." God works in mysterious ways, and apparently annoying ones too, because Nigel turned up and was saved a few weeks later—because God turned up.

On the day we distributed leaflets, Jeff told us that he wouldn't be able to join us. Jeff was in his sixties, but he volunteered to take the biggest neighborhood made up of 350 houses on his own later. "But I won't be able to do it in one day." He laughed. I probably wouldn't either. "I'll spread it out over a couple of days, but I'll get it done this week."

I don't know when Jeff went out to distribute those bad boys, but one of the leaflets was aimed straight at the Achilles heel of a woman named Carol. It soared out over the masses lodged straight into her heart. You see, Carol had terminal uterine cancer and was in hospice awaiting her final breath. Two Christians who worked with Carol had been afraid of her because of her rapier wit, and had decided to visit her in the hospital, thinking, *What's there to lose now?* In her hospital bed, Carol listened bitterly as they unfolded the gospel to her. Feeling that they'd failed, they asked if they could pray for her. She reluctantly shrugged and said, "You might as well." They prayed for Carol. Not just that God would save her soul, but that He'd heal her body. And He did.

The next morning the doctor ran a test and asked, "Do you believe in miracles?"

"No," Carol said.

"Well you just got one, regardless." The doctor ran some more tests and discharged her within a few days. The day that she got home, Carol was confused and a bit scared. Having just been released from a metaphorical death row, she had questions. Lying flat on her back on the sofa, she looked up at the ceiling and said, "I don't know who you are—he, she, or it. But tell me what you want from me."

Less than five minutes later, our leaflet came through the mail slot on her front door. She arose to go get it, thinking it might be a sign, and when she read the leaflet advertising the church starting up in her neighborhood that Sunday, the hackles rose on her neck. Out of all of the days that Jeff could have distributed that flyer, and it arrived at that moment. That was the start of God turning up. It gets better.

That Sunday morning I was preaching on Jesus saying that He was the Good Shepherd. I sarcastically pointed out the "profound truth" that John 9 came before John 10. I explained that before this conversation about the Good Shepherd, there had been a guy who had been healed of blindness. The Pharisees had asked him who healed him, and he could only respond, "I don't know. I was blind—I never saw him. Maybe you can tell me. All I know is that it must have been from God." As I was preaching, I kept noticing a woman in her sixties glaring at me with what appeared to be trembling rage. Funny how easy it is to mistake fear for anger. She was terrified. She was coming face-to-face with God, and He was telling her not to be afraid, that He was the Good Shepherd and that she would hear His voice and trust it.

She did. Carol came to know Jesus and walked with Him in ways that humbled me at times. She was a fireball of a woman and quite a character. Many a time Carol peeled the wallpaper off the wall with some of her observations and northern English humor. God turned up supernaturally in Carol's life, and therefore in ours. We were allowed to be a part of what God was doing in the world, simply because we turned up and partnered with what the Spirit was doing. Perhaps that's all it is. I may say that God turns up, but perhaps it's the other way around. Perhaps like Jesus said, "My Father is working until now, and I am working" (John 5:17). This time, we got to be a part of it—because we turned up.

That's the type of stuff that happens when both of you turn up. You can't sell it, package it, or reproduce it. Like the wind, He blows where and how He pleases. I just want to be there when it happens.

Another time, I'd freshly come back from America. A college student had brought a friend of his who clearly had designs on getting one of the girls into bed. As I talked to the girl about baptism in the front hallway, this guy sauntered up and listened politely. He interjected, "I'd like to get baptized too." Although I didn't know this guy from Adam, the Spirit whispered to my heart, *He just wants to get her into bed.* So, as I talked, I said, "Great. Baptism signifies the change in your life that happens as you become one with Christ. He took your life upon Him at the cross, and the old you died. When you become a Christian, the new you comes alive, and you take His place as the Spirit now lives in you. It signifies that you've been spiritually raised from the dead, and you live a new life."

"What do you mean?" he asked me dully.

"Well, for example, it means that the change in you is so great that you wouldn't ever try to get her into bed." I pointed at the girl.

The guy turned a million shades of red like a cartoon character. *Won't see him again*, I thought. Next week, he turned up again and interrupted the meeting to say that he "felt God."

"Neat," I said, and we continued to worship.

A little while into the meeting, Jeff interrupted the prayer time and said to him, "So and so, I just feel like you're supposed to put your trust in Jesus tonight, and confess to Him."

I was gob-smacked. I had been sitting there feeling that precise thing but didn't know quite how to say it. I told the guy that although this wasn't usually how we did things, I was feeling that he needed to get saved. Suddenly, this guy who had never been to church in his life, or ever heard a sermon, blurted out in the middle of the meeting through broken sobs, "I'm sorry, God! I'm so sorry for the things I've done. I feel so dirty—please make me clean. Please forgive me!" It was beautiful, and it was totally, completely, and 100 percent an act of God. I felt like selling hot dogs, popcorn, and giant foam fingers, because in that room that night we were all spectators enjoying the show.

That guy became like a little brother to me, and his salvation set a whole row of dominoes off. One by one they fell, until the gospel had gone through the whole lot of them. One night, we were baptizing one of them and the Spirit of God was so thick, I stood in the water and actually began to get afraid. God was in the house, and we could all feel His presence. Two drug-addicted construction workers were there to watch their kid sister get baptized, and they became overwhelmed by the presence of God. One was saved that night, and the other months later. Another college student got saved as a result of that night from watching his friend get baptized, and more were saved at his baptism.

How can I replicate that? How can anybody?

William Temple summed it up when he said, "When I pray, coincidences happen; when I don't, they don't."

You do still expect God to turn up, don't you?

UNQUALIFIED QUALIFICATIONS

All of this is simply to tell you the importance of the real and ready presence of God in our midst, because we can't duplicate, replicate, or fabricate any of this without Him turning up. I'm not saying God doesn't, can't, or won't use you if you don't experience what I'm talking about. God has used me when I'm good, bad, and ugly. What I'm saying is that there is more power, and that this generation desperately needs to see it.

If you're thinking, "Man, I'd like to see God working in my life," it all starts by telling Him that. You don't have to be good enough, smart enough, or holy enough.

God uses knuckleheads. Look at me as proof. When we were planting Pillar, the biggest joke was that God could use me at all. When stuff went down, I walked around with a half-smirk on my face, thinking it was a pretty funny practical joke that God was playing on the people around me. At that time, I was pretty messed up. My mind kept going back to Peter telling the gawking crowds, "Men of Israel, why do you marvel at this? Or why look so intently at us, as though by our own power or godliness we had made this man walk?" (Acts 3:12 NKJV). I like that. Peter said, "as though by our own … godliness." I can't make people walk, save a soul, or make a seed grow.

Paul used a gardening analogy to communicate the same truth. He sowed and watered like Mr. Green Jeans on speed, but at the end of the day he couldn't make a single blade of grass grow no matter how hard he tried with his mental powers. The growing department belongs to God. People who think God uses them because they are godly can't be trusted to glorify God. They start hogging all the glory from Jesus and try to upstage Him. When that happens, the Holy Spirit has to back off. Suddenly, your purposes are at cross-purposes with the Spirit. You've started to glorify self, and He can't be party to that. God opposes the proud but gives grace to the humble.

In Acts 1:8, Jesus told a bunch of knuckleheads that they needed power to see the kingdom of God expand. The whole book is about what the Spirit of God can do with and through weaklings. Pathetic, cowardly, misguided weaklings. Look at the disciples. I mean, would you have seriously hired any of them if you were Jesus? Yet they were carefully chosen by the Father after a night of prayer and fasting.

Good thing you're not Jesus. You wouldn't have picked you.

Here's some more good news: Jesus is still looking for people He can turn the flame thrower on and set them and their surroundings ablaze. Any knuckleheads out there?

Those flames alighting atop the heads of the apostles on Pentecost were there to illustrate what was about to happen.

Because fire spreads.

Flame on!

11

EARTH: THE FINAL FRONTIER

The time of my departure has come. I have fought the good fight.

Paul, 2 Timothy 4:6–7

*I pray that when I die, all hell will have a party to
celebrate the fact that I am no longer in the fight.*

C. T. Studd

I made a pilgrimage to save this human race.

Modern English, "I Melt With You"

I wanna be an airborne Ranger!

John Bender, *The Breakfast Club*

Well, the fat lady is about to open her pie hole, which means this is almost over.

A group of Spurgeon's sermons were collected in a volume called *The Teachings of Nature in the Kingdom of Grace*. It is phenomenal. It examines weeds, seeds, and gardening deeds. At each stage, he identified in Puritan fashion what God is saying to man through the design of the natural world around us, through which we see His divine attributes. Similarly, the Bible speaks about planting seeds that produce a tree, which in turn produces fruit. Each piece of fruit is a package—a package containing multiple seeds for planting.

Why did God hardwire each piece of fruit for multiplication, yet when we bear fruit, we see it as the endgame? If we were following God's design for fruit, we'd know that like fruit, churches are packages for spreading seeds—for planting multiple churches. One seed becomes a tree, which becomes another seed factory.

Stetzer used the title *Viral Churches* to communicate this idea. Jesus said it this way: "in one case a hundredfold, in another sixty, and in another thirty" (Matt. 13:23). That's what disciples do—they reproduce.

Isn't that what the Great Commission was all about anyway? Making disciples?

Isn't it odd that the Son of God spent the majority of His three years of earthly ministry investing primarily in twelve lost causes instead of filling stadiums?

Staying focused is a challenge, but if you keep breaking off church-planting seeds, seeking like a piece of fruit to be a seed-bearing package, then you'll have no problem. Whether it's the birds, wind, or weather, something will carry those seeds to another destination where they will be needed. Stuff doesn't grow where it's not needed, and this world is one needy place.

The times demand men and women who are called to spread the seeds of the gospel by investing in, traveling with, and turning loose the next generation of apostolic teams.

When I made preparations to leave Pillar, I looked around the table and shared with my team. I was convinced that a couple of the young men would want to take it, but nothing doing. They looked at me blankly, and said, "We want to plant." That kinda sucked in a way, but it also demonstrated that the core values had been successfully instilled in them. Lee Iacocca once said that you know that you've finally arrived when they hand you the key to the executive restroom. I'd say it's more like staring in the eyes of the guys you thought would be following in your wake for sure, only to find that you've reproduced yourself so well, they can't wait to go out and cut new channels through the waves for the kingdom.

Churches should be part Mogwai. Multiplication is so hard-wired into their DNA that all you have to do is accidentally spill water on them and they pop out five more furry little church plant balls.

As the church begins to rediscover its A-Team roots, first-century networking stapled with the power of the Holy Spirit will rip the world a new one for the gospel.

THE COMING DARK

When guys like Hal Lindsey talk about the end of the world, you think "faded paperback at a garage sale," but when guys like John Piper talk about the end of the world, you startle awake.

It's happening. You can feel it. Like Galadriel says at the beginning of *The Fellowship of the Rings* film, "The world is changed. I feel it in the water. I feel it in the earth. I smell it in the air. Much that once was, is lost—for none now live who remember it."[1]

The world is changing, and God is raising up a generation who are returning to the Scriptures for the final push of God's glory in these last days. Regarding the end times, the Puritans held the belief that in earth's final days, while sin corrupted this world to unseen horrors, the church would shine its very brightest. The church is getting ready to be ignited again in a blaze of selfless sacrifice in imitation of our greatest apostle and forerunner, who was sent here to kick off the revolution against the tyranny of self, sin, and Satan.

GOING POSTAL MODERN

Are you ready to spark a revolution in the ranks of the church and wake the sleeping giant? Are you ready to light the torches that spark a thousand points of light? Are you ready to rise to the challenge of the incoming second wave of the Dark Ages, like Ridley and Latimer at the dawn of the Reformation, and "light a candle that can never be put out"?

It's gonna cost you.

If we'll simply believe Jesus, embrace the cross, and turn our backs on the crowds, somehow new life will spring up out of our death. The blood of the martyrs was the seed of the church, but I believe that this also applies to what the apostle Paul meant when he said, "We die daily." As we lay down our lives for the unchurched in our midst and go on co-missional ventures in the footsteps of Jesus, He'll spring up new resurrection power in the kingdom of God until its borders expand like never before.

That's what will happen when the church has the reform from ground zero. Simply put, ground zero is where the church was two thousand years ago. As we revisit our roots and raze our sand-built edifices in favor of the firm bedrock of our apostolic roots, God will build a church equipped to face the final push for Christ's glory in the coming dark.

I firmly believe that God will pour out His Spirit in these dark days like never before, but new wine requires new wineskins.

During David's dynasty, more ground was taken in battle for Israel's borders than at any other time before or after. It was called the golden age of Israel's history. Could this be the generation known as the golden age of the church? It's not too late.

True, these are dark times, but like pretty little Esther you've come into the kingdom for such a time as this, my uglies. In dark times, you just gotta do what Bruce Cockburn said and "kick at the darkness till it bleeds daylight."[2]

We've got our marching orders.

We've been shown how the troops should form up.

We've got a Captain who boldly goes before us to lead the charge.

All that's left now is to climb out from the trenches and take "No Man's Land."

Every church reformation has turned the tide of battle so that the church was charging through the barbed wire on the offensive, instead of hiding in foxholes on the defensive, praying that the shelling would stop.

Church Zero is a call to reformation and nothing short of it.

All church reformers shared one thing in common with every man who has ever spilled his blood on the field of battle; they valued victory for the cause more than their own lives.

In a life-and-death struggle, victory is all that matters.

William Wallace stirred the troops before they took the field. I pray that this book has stirred your soul to take to the field and fight!

I believe that the church's final hour will be its finest hour if it has the stomach for waging war to drive back the gates of hell.

To inspire you for that final push, I've taken liberties with Winston Churchill's "Finest Hour" speech that he delivered upon the fall of France to Hitler; I've changed the context from Britain facing the onslaught of Nazi aggression to the kingdom of Christ making its stand against the gates of hell on the postmodern battlefield.

Upon this battle depends the survival of Christian civilization.
Upon it depends our own life,
And the long continuity of our churches and the kingdom.
Satan knows that he will have to break us on this field or lose the war.
If we can stand up to him, all humanity may be free,
And the life of the world may move forward
Into broad, sunlit uplands.

But if we fail, then the whole world,

Including our churches,

Including all we have known and cared for,

Will sink into the abyss of a new Dark Age

Made more sinister, and perhaps more protracted,

By the lights of perverted science.

Let us therefore brace ourselves to our duties,

And so bear ourselves

That if the kingdom of Christ and His church

Last for a thousand years,

Men will say:

"This was their finest hour."

NOTES

CHAPTER 1

1. Apparently, *ain't* still ain't a word. Even if you use an apostrophe. I always thought my teachers would live to eat their words. My spell-checker took issue with it. Apparently they are still right.
2. C. T. Studd, quoted in Norman Grubb, *C. T. Studd, Cricketer and Pioneer* (Fort Washington, PA: CLC Publications, 2008), 145.
3. It is often argued that Paul started more than twenty churches, if Acts and the epistles are carefully examined. Paul was indirectly responsible for the multiple churches that Titus planted in Crete. There appeared to be a church in Athens after Luke wrote that some believed. Fourteen to twenty plants is impressive in only eleven years.
4. This quote comes from a personal recording of Keith Green speaking at one of his concerts. The context of the quote was that Green had been walking around the festival and had seen lots of booths selling "Jesus junk."
5. Radiohead, "How to Disappear Completely," *Kid A* © 2000 Parlophone.

CHAPTER 2

1. That's the bony part of your butt.
2. C. Peter Wagner, *Church Planting for Greater Harvest* (Ventura, CA: Regal, 1990), 11.
3. Eusebius, *Ecclesiastical History*, quoted in David Ollerton, *Ministry on the Move* (Llandysul, Wales: Newid, 2007), 12.
4. Eusebius, *Ecclesiastical History* (Grand Rapids, MI: Baker, 1989), 123.
5. I know that some will try and argue that it was right there all along, but it definitely wasn't mainstream. If it had been, the Reformation wouldn't have been such a big deal.

6. If you've only been to Disney World, you have no idea what I'm talking about.

7. The only way in which Paul will allow that he is "inferior" to the Twelve is when he said, "For I am the least of the apostles, unworthy to be called an apostle, because I persecuted the church of God" (1 Cor. 15:9).

8. Consequently, after this, the Twelve never replaced their number again. They'd fulfilled their role of witnessing to the twelve tribes of Israel.

9. Wayne Grudem, *Systematic Theology* (Leicester: IVP, 1994), 906.

10. Erroll Hulse, "John Calvin and His Missionary Enterprise," *Reformation Today* 4 (1998), http://reformed-theology.org/html/issue04/calvin.htm (accessed March 1, 2012).

11. John Calvin, *Institutes of Religion*, IV.III.4.

CHAPTER 3

1. Stephen E. Ambrose, *D-Day* (New York: Touchstone, 1994), 211.

2. David Garrison, *Church Planting Movements* (Midlothian, VA: Wigtake, 2004), 28.

3. Alan Hirsch, *The Permanent Revolution* (San Francisco: Jossey-Bass, 2012), 3.

4. *Aliens*, directed by James Cameron (Los Angeles: Twentieth Century-Fox, 1986).

CHAPTER 4

1. Iain H. Murray, *The Puritan Hope* (Edinburgh: Banner, 1971), 141.

2. Arthur Wallis quoted in David Ollerton, *Ministry on the Move* (Llandysul, Wales: Newid, 2008), 15.

3. Acts 13–14. The four churches planted were in Pisidian Antioch, Iconium, Lystra, and Derbe.

4. Geraint Fielder, *Grace, Grit, and Gumption* (Bridgend: Christian Focus, 2000), 9.

5. Although most people associate the revival with Evan Roberts, it was the preaching of Seth Joshua, the most prominent of the Forward Movement Church planters, that sparked Evan Roberts during a youth rally.

6. A. W. Tozer, *Keys to the Deeper Life* (Grand Rapids, MI: Zondervan, 1988), 45–46.

7. Alan Hirsch and Michael Frost, *The Shaping of Things to Come* (Peabody, MA: Hendrickson, 2003), 195.

8. *The Matrix*, directed by Andy Wachowski and Larry Wachowski (Burbank, CA: Warner Brothers Pictures, 1999).

CHAPTER 5

1. Frank Houghton, "Facing a Task Unfinished," Overseas Missionary Fellowship, 1930. Used with permission.

2. Keith Green, "Asleep in the Light," *No Compromise* © 1978 Sparrow Records.

3. "Earnestness: Its Marring and Maintenance," *The Spurgeon Fellowship Journal Historical Reflection* (2007): 8.

4. John Wesley, *The Words of the Reverend John Wesley, A. M.* (New York: J. Emory and B. Waugh, 1831), 178.

CHAPTER 6

1. Carl Douglas, "Kung-Fu Fighting," *Kung Fu Fighting and Other Great Love Songs* © 1974 20th Century Fox Records.

2. Sosipater and Sopater might be the same guy, just as Silas could be the same as Silvanus.

3. Generally the network spans a two-hour travel radius.

4. William Arthur, *The Life of Gideon Ousely* (London: Wesleyan Conference Office, 1876), 47, 65.

CHAPTER 7

1. Martin Luther King Jr., "Letter from a Birmingham Jail," April 16, 1963, http://www.africa.upenn.edu/Articles_Gen/Letter_Birmingham.html (accessed October 23, 2012).

2. Jim Petersen, *Church Without Walls* (Colorado Springs: NavPress, 1992), 215–16.

3. David Ollerton, *Ministry on the Move* (Llandysul, Wales: Newid 2008), 25.

4. Helen Lee, "Missional Shift or Drift?" *Leadership Journal,* Fall 2008, 27.

5. Richard Baxter, *The Reformed Pastor* (London: Banner of Truth Trust, 1974), 76–78.

6. U2, "If God Will Send His Angels," *Pop* © 1997 Island.

7. "Rebecca," quoted in Thom S. Rainer, and Jess W. Rainer, *The Millennials* (Nashville: B&H, 2011), 267.

8. U2, "Vertigo," *How to Dismantle an Atomic Bomb* © 2004 Island.

9. John Krakauer, *Into the Wild* (New York: Anchor, 1997), 57.

10. Basil Miller, *William Carey: The Father of Modern Missions* (Minneapolis: Bethany House Publishers, 1980), 37.

11. F. Deaville Walker, *William Carey. Missionary Pioneer and Statesman* (Chicago: Moody Press, 1925), 54. See the recent discussion of this event by Brian Stanley, *The History of the Baptist Missionary Society 1792–1992* (Edinburgh: T & T Clark, 1992), 6–7.

CHAPTER 8

1. Dibin Samuel, "Mahatma Gandhi and Christianity," *Christianity Today*, August 14, 2008, http://in.christiantoday.com/articledir/print.htm?id=2837.

2. Cathy Lynn Grossman, "Survey: Non-attendees Find Faith Outside Church," *USA Today*, January 23, 2008, http://www.usatoday.com/news/religion/2008-01-09-unchurched-survey_N.htm.

3. Coldplay, "Every Teardrop is a Waterfall," Mylo Xyloto © 2011 Parlophone.

CHAPTER 9

1. E. Stanley Jones, *The Reconstruction of the Church—On What Pattern?* (Nashville: Abingdon, 1970), 109.

2. Jones, 109.